EXPLORING SILENT READING FLUENCY

STANFORD E. TAYLOR, M.A.
Founder, Chairman
Reading Plus®/Taylor Associates/Communications, Inc.

Stanford E. Taylor is the founder of Taylor Associates and principal designer of the Reading Plus® system. Prior to establishing Taylor Associates, Mr. Taylor was founder and president of Educational Development Laboratories, Inc. (EDL/McGraw-Hill) and subsequently Instructional/Communications Technology, Inc.

A pioneer in the introduction and use of technology to improve reading/listening in the classroom, Mr. Taylor designed, manufactured and distributed a variety of reading improvement devices, initiated the concept of the reading lab, and introduced the first mobile reading lab.

He previously served as a reading technology supervisor in the Bethpage, New York schools, a reading technology instructor at Wagner College in Staten Island, New York, director of the Amackassin School in Blairstown, New Jersey, director of the Taylor Center for Reading Research in Huntington, New York, and comprehension skills editor for *Popular Science* magazine. He is an honorary member of The International Reading Association and the author of the National Education Association publication, *What Research Says to the Classroom Teacher about Listening.* Mr. Taylor has published numerous articles for American Education Research Association journals and contributed to the publication of over 300 books and instructional programs in the area of reading.

EXPLORING SILENT READING FLUENCY

FLUENCY

Its Nature and Development

By

STANFORD E. TAYLOR, M.A.

Taylor Associates/Communications

With Contributions by

S. Jay Samuels, ED.D.

University of Minnesota

Timothy Rasinski, PH.D.

Kent State University

Alexandra Spichtig, M.A.

Taylor Associates/Communications

CHARLES C THOMAS • PUBLISHER, LTD.
Springfield • Illinois • U.S.A.

Published and Distributed Throughout the World by

CHARLES C THOMAS • PUBLISHER, LTD.
2600 South First Street
Springfield, Illinois 62704

© 2011 by CHARLES C THOMAS • PUBLISHER, LTD.

ISBN 978-0-398-08676-3 (paper)
ISBN 978-0-398-08677-0 (ebook)

Library of Congress Catalog Card Number: 2011016997

With THOMAS BOOKS *careful attention is given to all details of manufacturing
and design. It is the Publisher's desire to present books that are satisfactory as to their
physical qualities and artistic possibilities and appropriate for their particular use.*
THOMAS BOOKS *will be true to those laws of quality that assure a good name
and good will.*

Printed in the United States of America
MM-R-3

Library of Congress Cataloging-in-Publication Data

Taylor, Stanford E. (Stanford Earl), 1927–
 Exploring silent reading fluency : its nature and development / by
Stanford E. Taylor ; with contributions by S. Jay Samuels . . . [et al.].
  p. cm.
 Includes bibliographical references and index.
 ISBN 978-0-398-08676-3 (pbk.) -- ISBN 978-0-398-08677-0 (ebook)
 1. Silent reading. I. Samuels, S. Jay. II. Title.

LB1050.55.T39 2011
372.45'4–dc23

                                        2011016997

CONTRIBUTORS

S. JAY SAMUELS, ED.D.

Professor
Department of Educational Psychology
University of Minnesota

Dr. S. Jay Samuels is a professor and reading researcher at the University of Minnesota. He is a recipient of numerous awards for his work in the field of reading, including the International Reading Association William S. Gray Citation of Merit for outstanding contributions to the field of reading (1987) and the National Reading Conference Oscar S. Causey Award for outstanding contributions to reading research (1985). He is a member of the Reading Hall of Fame and the National Institutes of Child Health and Human Development National Reading Panel.

Before joining the University of Minnesota's faculty, Dr. Samuels taught for more than a decade in elementary schools in New York and California. He currently teaches courses in Reading Fluency and Educational Psychology, among others. Dr. Samuels is a frequent contributor to leading reading research journals. He has published hundreds of articles, and has edited or co-edited numerous reading publications.

Dr. Samuels' interests include the development of materials and methods for improving word recognition, fluency, and comprehension. He also investigates how to facilitate young readers' understanding of moral themes as well as how to measure reading fluency.

TIMOTHY RASINSKI, PH.D.

Professor of Literacy
Kent State University

Timothy Rasinski is a professor of literacy education at Kent State University. He recently served a three-year term on the International Reading Association's board of directors.

Dr. Rasinski has served as co-editor of *The Reading Teacher,* the most widely read journal of literacy education. He has also served as co-editor of the *Journal of Literacy Research,* and is a past president of the College Reading Association. He was a recipient of the College Reading Association's A. B. Herr and Laureate Awards for his scholarly and lifetime contributions to literacy education. Prior to joining the Kent State faculty, Dr. Rasinski taught literacy education at the University of Georgia. He also taught for several years as an elementary and middle school teacher, as well as a Title I teacher in rural Nebraska.

Dr. Rasinski has written more than 150 articles, and has authored, co-authored, or edited more than 50 books or curriculum programs on reading education. His research on reading has been cited by the National Reading Panel and has been published in journals such as *Reading Research Quarterly, The Reading Teacher, Reading Psychology,* and the *Journal of Educational Research.* He recently led a team that wrote the chapter on fluency for Volume IV of the *Handbook of Reading Research.*

His scholarly interests include reading fluency and word study, reading in the elementary and middle grades, and readers who struggle.

ALEXANDRA SPICHTIG, M.A.

Director of Product Development
Taylor Associates/Communications

Alexandra Spichtig manages and coordinates all product development for Reading Plus®, directing the people and processes that enhance the Reading Plus®

system.

Before joining the company in 1997, Alexandra was an educator in Switzerland, where she held positions as a classroom teacher and educational committee board member. She has a bachelor's degree in education from Cantonal Teacher's Training College in Lucerne, Switzerland, and also has a master's degree in teaching English as a second and foreign language from St. Michael's College in Winooski, Vermont.

Alexandra is currently working toward a doctoral degree in instructional design for online learning. She is writing her dissertation on the effects of electronic text presentation formats on silent reading fluency and proficiency development.

This book is dedicated to the memory of my father, Earl A. Taylor, whose pioneering work inspired my lifelong study of silent reading fluency and development of products to help improve reading proficiency. In addition, the book is dedicated to my wife, Dorothea Taylor, whose support over the years has been the foundation of my achievements in reading research, design, and development.

PREFACE

Our common primary goal as reading educators is to improve reading instruction. To do that, we must embrace the advantages computer technology can offer when planning a curriculum for students that will successfully develop proficiency and fluency in silent reading.

It is evident from statistics that our nation's students need to improve their reading proficiency. While progress has been made in National Assessment of Educational Progress (NAEP) scores since 2005, the relatively low scores of fourth and eighth graders at present, the disparity of these scores between affluent and less privileged students, the high dropout rate, and the discontent of many students with traditional classroom learning clearly indicate that something different must be done.

It is encouraging that a growing number of research reports show computer learning can significantly improve student achievement in reading. These reports strongly suggest a reconsideration of what might be best provided by a teacher and what might be more appropriately delivered by computer technology. Studies of the use of computer learning in "before the bell," after school, and home study programs are increasing. These findings will undoubtedly stimulate changes that will affect student appraisal, instruction, management, and achievement. A strong argument for computer learning is also emerging with regard to teacher limitations. Certain aspects of the reading process simply cannot be directed by a teacher, nor controlled by a student, and so must be developed with the assistance of computer technology, as described in this book.

It is generally agreed, I think, by all educators that reading proficiency is the key to success in all learning and that silent reading is the dominant form of learning. Therefore, more attention must be focused on the best means to develop silent reading proficiency, which encompasses a multitude of skills needed to achieve ease and comfort, adequate reading rates, comprehension competency, and vocabulary enhancement in reading.

It is the goal of this book to provide unique and helpful information to reading and curriculum specialists who are looking for ways to improve the silent reading proficiency of their students. While the background information is, at times, somewhat technical, the recommendations as to the skill areas that require improvement as well as the computer techniques that can produce this improvement will prove extremely helpful in planning for a more comprehensive reading proficiency course of instruction.

Reading and tutoring centers will naturally be interested in both the diagnostic eye-movement recording techniques as well as the web-based practice techniques available through computer technology. The ability for clients to use this silent reading development technology at home, beyond usual clinic hours, is certainly an advantage in terms of reading remediation.

Reading researchers should also be intrigued by the comprehensive description of the silent reading process as well as the effects of oral reading on the development of proficiency in silent reading. Especially helpful should be the information revealed through eye-movement recordings about the many subliminal factors involved in the process of reading, as well as the changes produced by today's web-based computer techniques to modify the basic visual/functional, perceptual, and information processing skills that comprise the silent reading process.

In addition, higher education curriculum directors may be interested in this book as recommended reading for graduate courses that cover what occurs during silent reading and what outcomes are possible with current reading practice programs using web-based computer technology. Such programs might also be of interest for their use with incoming freshmen who need to improve their silent reading proficiency to deal with the more extensive and higher-level content they will encounter in their post-secondary education.

Classroom teachers may be particularly interested in the chapters that describe what has and can be done in classrooms and labs to improve silent reading proficiency.

The purpose of this book is multifaceted. It discusses the complexity of the reading process and calls attention to the fact that some of the more basic visual/functional, perceptual, and information processing skills that constitute proficient reading are not addressed in most core or basal reading programs today. A brief overview of the contents of the book is as follows:

Chapter 1–"The Dynamic Activity of Reading." Describes the visual/perceptual process of silent reading in terms of the seeing, perceiving, understanding, and divergent thinking functions that comprise this process.

Chapter 2–"Eye-Movement Recording of the Reading Process." Provides an introduction to the only means of analyzing the dynamic activity of reading and describes the detailed information that can be derived about a reader's efficiency or fluency in silent reading. While eye-movement recording may not be possible with all students, certainly the reading process of struggling readers should be examined to determine the instructional practices that will best meet their needs. The term "struggling reader" applies not only to students who exhibit low achievement, but also to better readers who read in a slow and labored manner. Building proficiency in all students so they can reach their true potential for proficient reading must be the goal of all reading instruction.

Chapter 3–"Technology's Role in Silent Reading Fluency Development." A brief history of the instructional devices that have been used over the past 80 years to both appraise and improve silent reading fluency. From this beginning, today's computer appraisal and reading development techniques have emerged.

Chapter 4–"Oculomotor Activity During Reading." A review of the manner in which word information is fed to the mind in silent reading in a relatively habitual manner. This process is conditioned by a reader's visual/perceptual processes that are fashioned in early reading and can only be effectively and directly altered by today's computerized reading development approaches.

Chapter 5–"Moving Toward Fluency in Silent Reading." Examines the effects of oral reading practice on the development of a student's oculomotor activity in silent reading. Oral reading practices are certainly helpful in terms of word recognition and realization of phrasing, but too much oral reading practice can produce detrimental effects on silent reading behavior. Therefore, a better balance is needed between oral reading fluency practice and silent reading fluency development as delivered by computer assisted instruction if proficiency in silent reading is to emerge.

Chapter 6–"Today's Technology to Develop Silent Reading Proficiency and Fluency." A description of an ideal computerized reading development system that can provide a more comprehensive approach to the development of silent reading fluency and proficiency.

Not only are these software techniques critical to the development of reading proficiency, an ideal practice system must also provide scaffolding of instruction to ensure more targeted individualized instruction for each student. Computer scaffolding goes far beyond what a teacher can provide, as instruction is adjusted step-by-step on the basis of a student's comprehension, rate, and lesson progress. Such instruction also goes far beyond what more reading practice alone can provide.

Now is the time for reading instruction to change and expand in regard to skill development. Computer technology along with teacher direction and traditional book reading can provide students with the means to more fully achieve reading proficiency. Change comes slowly in the educational system, but new research is demonstrating the vital role computer technology can play in reading instruction. Since changes in most computer programs will be made steadily throughout each year based on extensive analysis of online student records, it is important to realize that studies of efficacy must be an ongoing process, year by year. What was done yesterday will be improved in the future and even greater student gains will result.

CONTENTS

EXPLORING SILENT READING FLUENCY

Chapter 1

THE DYNAMIC ACTIVITY OF READING

A Model of the Reading Process

STANFORD E. TAYLOR

This chapter will describe the approximate 30 functions, many quite sub-liminal in nature, that interact during each second of reading. The stages of seeing and perceiving are not typically considered in most reading development programs today. Basal reading programs tend to focus more on phonics and the understanding phases of reading, leaving students on their own to master many of the most basic skills involved in word recognition and processing of information. Undoubtedly, this lack of attention to the development of the subliminal visual and perceptual skills accounts for the considerable increase in struggling readers today as well as the slow reading rates of even better students. Because the reading process is so complex, questions will logically arise such as how to evaluate the efficiency of these processes and how to best improve these functions to increase reading efficiency or fluency in silent reading.

In the chapters to follow, eye-movement recording of the reading process is explored. Additionally, the technology that has been employed over the years to improve these processes will be described, culminating with a review of the opportunities to use today's computer software techniques in a highly scaffolded manner to provide the most individualized program of reading efficiency development for each student that will lead to increased enjoyment of reading, more thorough comprehension, and enhanced success in all study and vocational tasks.

For the purpose of this discussion, the process of reading, as shown in the following diagram, is divided into four steps: seeing, perceiving, understanding and/or reacting, and elaborative and/or divergent thinking.

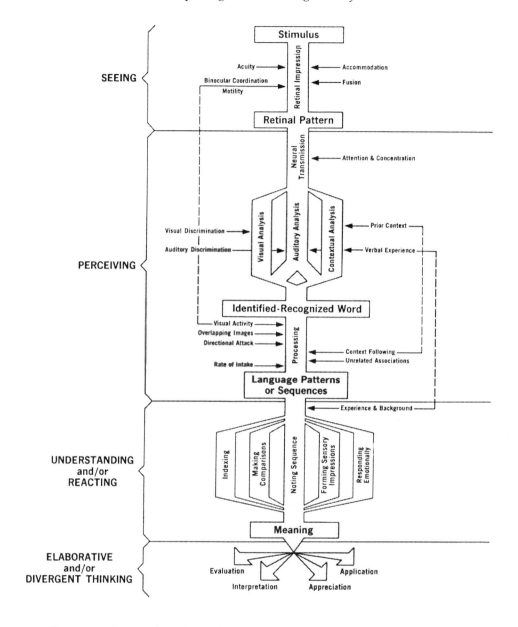

Seeing refers to the physiological stage of the reading process in which the light reflected from the page that contains the print is transformed by retinal activity into neural transmissions that are dispatched to the brain.

Perceiving refers to the psychological process of becoming aware of the orthography or letter configuration of words. During this stage the reader first identifies and then recognizes printed words through the avenues of visual analysis, auditory analysis, and/or association with meaning. The reader then processes these words in a manner that permits him or her to become aware of their sequence and the language patterns they constitute.

Understanding and/or reacting refers to a continuation of the psychological process in which word sequences are accepted in light of the reader's experience and background and are translated into meaning through one or more processes of thought: indexing, making comparisons, noting sequence, forming sensory impressions, and responding emotionally.

Elaborative and/or divergent thinking occurs after the reader has established meaning and starts to evaluate, interpret, appreciate, and apply what has been read.

In presenting this diagram, it is acknowledged that the factors involved in the reading process may vary at times in the order in which they occur and will change in their importance from one reading situation to another. Further, many of these factors, while depicted separately, may act in combination or simultaneously.

SEEING

The Stimulus

The reading process starts with the stimulus of the reflected light striking the retina of the reader's eye. When considering the nature of the stimulus in reading, one is concerned fundamentally with aspects of legibility of print. It is sufficient to say that legibility is dependent on the contrast between the print and its background (as presented by Luckiesh & Moss in 1941), the amount of illumination striking the page and being reflected by it (as cited by Tinker in 1963), the typeface, the amount of leading (as determined by Buckingham in 1931), and other such factors that affect the quality and quantity of the reflected light impinging on the retina of the eye. Since the reader has little control over the nature of the stimulus (except control over illumination during reading), we shall concern ourselves in this discussion with what happens when the stimulus is presented to the retina of the eye and what happens from that point forward, as depicted in the following diagram.

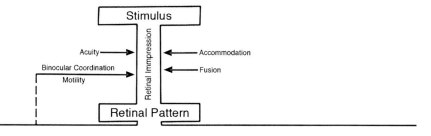

The Retinal Impression

The first factors to be considered are those that affect the quality of the retinal impression.

Acuity (resolving power) is the ability to see clearly and distinctly. Almost all educators will agree that adequate visual acuity is a prerequisite to effective word recognition and success in reading. However, many schools today are still satisfied with a routine screening using the Snellen distance vision test, which will detect those students who are myopic (nearsighted) but will "pass" most students who are hyperopic (farsighted) and many others with more subtle visual handicaps involving aniseikonia (difference in the size of the same visual impression by the two eyes), astigmatism (imperfect perceived image resulting from irregularities in the cornea of the eye), etc.

Consider those who are hyperopic. In the hyperopic eye, the image falls behind the retina when reading at near point, as shown in the following illustration.

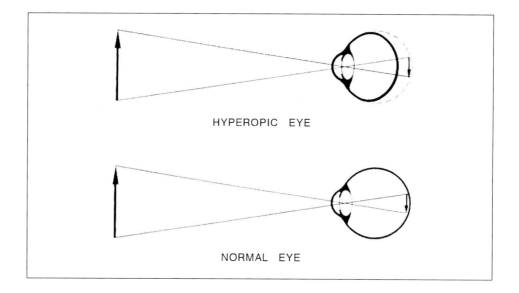

This condition would cause words to appear somewhat blurred and poorly defined if a child does not possess adequate reserves of accommodation in order to bring print back to proper or desired focus.

Hyperopia is a state through which most children pass, unfortunately at an age (up to seven or eight) critical to their development of visual discrimination and the acquisition of a basic sight vocabulary.

E. A. Taylor (1959) reported more cases of hyperopia in failing students than those who achieved reasonable success in their studies. H. M. Robinson

(1958), in discussing visual defects and reading difficulties, stated that more poor readers than good readers have been found to be hyperopic.

Accommodation is the ability of the eye to focus or adjust in order to bring an image into sharp focus. The eyes of a reader should adjust almost instantaneously to the reading distance. E. A. Taylor (1959), however, found that many children experiencing difficulty with reading exhibited sluggish focus. Some of these children required 30 to 60 seconds for a change of focus when looking up at the teacher and then back at their books. In addition, he found that the two eyes of many children change focus at different rates, which results in a certain amount of disorientation. Poor accommodation also poses a problem as a student moves his or her eyes from one fixation position to another fixation position.

In judging the adequacy of a student's acuity and accommodation, the first recommendation is a thorough examination by a vision specialist. If this is not possible, the use of a comprehensive visual screening device will help detect those students with the greatest visual handicaps, many of which can be corrected with glasses or visual training.

Fusion represents a state of single vision in which the images from the two eyes are merged with sufficient quality to be realized as one image only. Binocular coordination is the capability of using the two eyes "as a team" in a manner of movement that is sufficiently coordinated to permit and maintain fusion and thus single vision during a dynamic process such as reading.

Kephart (1960), in his study of 220 school children in grades 3 through 12, found that 4 out of every 10 lacked adequate visual skills for suitable academic progress. H. M. Robinson (1958) stated, "The visual conditions that appear most significant for reading are eye coordination difficulties involving depth perception, visual fusion, and lateral and vertical eye muscle balance. These problems in eye coordination raise, in turn, suspicions of something inadequate in the neurological controls of the eye, rather than the eye itself."

In a number of surveys conducted by E. A. Taylor of the Reading and Study Skills Center of New York from 1943 to 1950, several thousand children referred to the Center as needing corrective and remedial help in reading were tested for binocular coordination. Within this group, 95 percent showed a lack of sufficient coordination and fusion to carry out reading and study tasks in a satisfactory manner.

To maintain single binocular vision and adequate fusion during the reading act, a reader must have, as a minimum, 13 to 19 diopters of convergence (ability to rotate the eyes toward the nose in order to achieve the impingement of a given image on corresponding retinal areas) at a reading distance of 13 inches, as shown in the following illustration, with an appropriate interaction of the divergence function (the opposing rotational function that allows the eyes to be held in effective balance during reading and usual viewing).

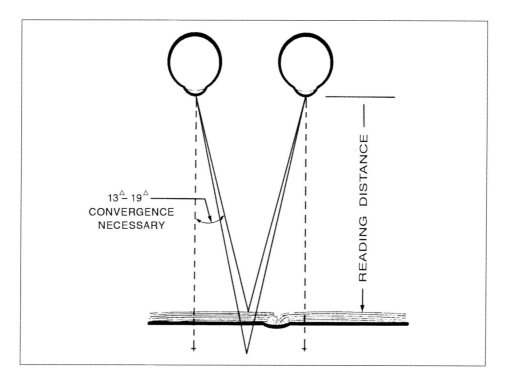

If the reader does not possess adequate binocular coordination, the word and letter shapes become less distinguishable, as the letters fluctuate between appearing to be single or double, as seen in the following example.

In addition, a lack of adequate reserve (an amount beyond the minimum requirement) of binocular control (perhaps 19 diopters of divergence and 39 diopters of convergence) causes the reader to struggle unconsciously to maintain single vision. This effort results in the expenditure of an extraordinary amount of energy that, for many, causes visual fatigue and/or a general feeling of discomfort. As a result, the reader's ability to attend and concentrate decreases, thus increasing his or her susceptibility to distraction.

According to Bartiss (2005), "Patients typically present themselves for testing and treatment as teenagers or in early adulthood, complaining of gradually worsening eye strain and periocular headache, blurred vision after brief periods of reading, and, sometimes, crossed diplopia (double vision) with near work." Fortunately, in most cases, convergence insufficiency, which is a problem with approximately 2.25 – 8.3 percent of the population, is very amenable to orthoptopics and vision therapy as stated in a report by Scheiman, Mitchell, Cotter, Cooper, Kulp, Rouse, Borsting, London, and Wensveen (2005).

During the 1960s and 1970s, a device called the Prism Reader, as shown in the following image, enabled vision specialists to measure the extent to which a person could maintain single binocular vision during the dynamic act of reading. Today, the easiest means of detecting binocular coordination handicaps is through eye-movement recording, which quickly detects differences in the performance of the two eyes during reading or with other visual tasks.

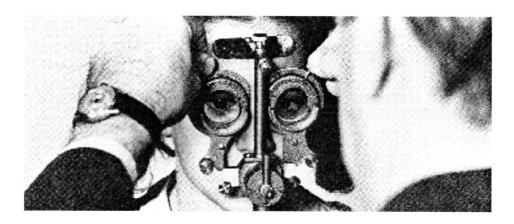

For use in school surveys, E. A. Taylor with Solan developed a checklist referred to as the Functional Readiness Questionnaire (1966). This questionnaire has now been replaced by the Student/Examiner Inventory Questionnaire, a similar series of questions that is used in conjunction with the Visagraph® eye-movement recording system developed by S. E. Taylor (1995). This questionnaire has been used quite successfully for years to detect the presence of binocular coordination and fusion difficulties.

Negative responses to a number of these questions, as shown in the following Student Inventory Questionnaire, could indicate that the student is experiencing visual/functional difficulties.

Reading Plus®
Visagraph® Student Inventory Questions

1. Do you like to read?
2. Do you get headaches when reading?
3. Can you read easily for 15 minutes?
4. Can you read easily for 30 minutes?
5. Can you read easily for 1 hour?
6. Can you read easily for 2 hours?
7. Do you get tired and sleepy when you read?
8. Do you study in short spurts?
9. Do your eyes get tired while reading?
10. Do your eyes get itchy while reading?
11. Do your eyes ever burn while reading?
12. Do your eyes get watery during reading?
13. Do the words in reading ever get muddy or blurred?
14. Do the letters in words double up or wiggle at times?
15. Do you find yourself saying the words to yourself during reading?
16. Do you have trouble understanding what you read?
17. Do you ever get car sick or headaches riding in a car?
18. Do you get a stiff neck or backache after reading?
19. Do you find your eyes bother you in sports such as baseball, basketball, tennis, or ping pong?
20. Do you feel your reading can be improved?

There is also a series of questions for the examiner, teacher, or parent to answer as shown in the following Teacher Inventory Questionnaire. Again, negative responses to a number of these questions can support the information furnished by the student inventory that might suggest visual/functional problems.

Reading Plus®
Visagraph® Teacher Inventory Questions

1. Is student's level of academic achievement satisfactory for his/her age and/or grade?
2. Has progress been satisfactory in reading?
3. Has the student repeated any grade?
4. Is the student interested in school?
5. Does the student fatigue easily during reading and study tasks?
6. Is there a tendency to study in spurts?
7. Is there a tendency for the student to be easily distracted during reading?
8. Does the student seem to be happy and well adjusted in the school environment?
9. Does the student attend school regularly?
10. Does he/she squint, blink, close or cover one eye at either close or distant viewing tasks?
11. During reading, is there a tendency to skip words, insert incorrect words or guess at words?
12. Does the student use a finger frequently to keep his/her place during reading?
13. Does the student frequently lose his/her place during reading?
14. Is there a tendency to tilt the head during reading?
15. Does the student draw in closer than 10 inches when reading?
16. Is there a tendency for one eye to turn in or out during reading?
17. Is there a considerable head movement during reading?
18. Is there a tendency to vocalize during reading?
19. Does the student develop red eyes or encrusted lids (exclusive of instances of infection)?
20. Does the student complain frequently about reading and study tasks being too time consuming?

Motility generally refers to the ease of facility with which a reader makes ocular rotations. Like coordination, this factor influences the comfort of the reader and the accuracy with which he or she makes fixations. In a study by S. E. Taylor and H. A. Robinson (1963), kindergarten and first-grade children were photographed with an eye-movement camera while performing certain ocular tasks. In one test, they were asked to move their eyes back and forth between two dots as rapidly as possible. Results of this test dramatically illustrated the difference in motility among children: in 15 seconds, some could make as many as 60 excursions, while others could affect only 8 excursions. Additionally, many children could not move their eyes without moving their heads. This condition prohibited 15 percent of them from being photographed on any of the tests in the study. In fact, the role of visual motility as a factor influencing success in reading has been pointed out by such early investigators as Bing (1964), Eames (1932), Good (1939), Gould, Henderson, and Scheele (1964), Imus, Rothney, and Baer (1938), Kephart (1960), H. M. Robinson and Huelsman, Jr. (1952), and E. A. Taylor (1966).

From all of these references, it becomes obvious that the ease and facility of eye rotation can determine, in great measure, the accuracy with which a reader will make saccadic excursions, fixate, and perceive, which will influence the level of fluency he or she will be able to achieve in silent reading.

The Retinal Pattern

Having considered the visual factors that could lessen the quality of the retinal impression, let us next consider what constitutes a retinal impression in the case of an emmetropic (normal) eye when accommodation and fusion are satisfactory.

The retinal impression is initiated when light reflects from the page, strikes the retina of the eye, and creates a pattern of stimulation on the foveal and peripheral areas.

The retina of the eye is composed of sensory cells called rods and cones. The sensory cells that react best to the form and shape of letters are the cones. The closer the cones are grouped together, the greater the resolution and, therefore, the greater the visual acuity. In the central retinal area, especially in the fovea centralis, the cones predominate even to the exclusion of the rods. Proceeding outward from the fovea, the number of cones diminishes, whereas the rods become more numerous. As a result, the print falling on the fovea of the eye will be quite clear and distinct, while the print extending out from the fixation point into the periphery will tend to be progressively less distinct. Thus, the number of letters that can be accurately perceived is quite limited.

The diagram that follows is based on the results of a study by Feinberg (1949), who determined the "fall-off" of acuity for the emmetropic eye.

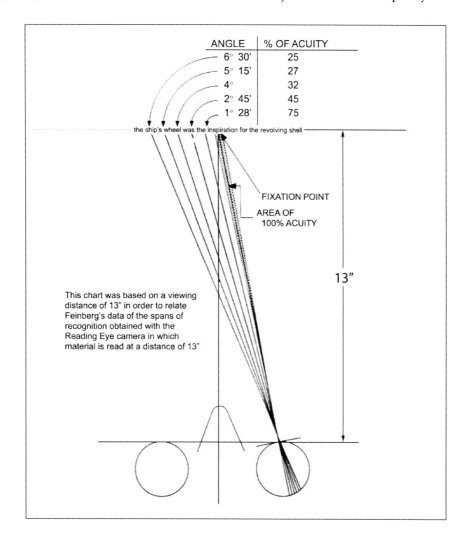

As a reader stops his or her eyes on a line of print, only four to five letters immediately around the fixation point are seen with 100 percent acuity. From this point of clearest vision outward in either direction, words and their letters are seen with steadily decreasing clarity. For example, portions of words that extend one-half inch beyond the fixation point are normally seen with less than 50 percent acuity. Should there be any visual impediments as a result of less than normal acuity, improper accommodation, or inadequate coordination and fixation, the clarity or distinctiveness of the words would be further reduced.

The study by Feinberg (1949) as well as findings by Legge, Cheung, Yu, Chung, Lee, and Owens (2007), explained, in part, why the span of recognition (the amount of words apprehended during a single fixation during continuous reading) is quite limited, up to one word for readers up to the high school level and seldom more than 2.5 words for an exceptionally skilled and mature reader.

PERCEIVING

When the reflected light from around the printed word strikes the retina of the eye, an electro-chemical change occurs, which in turn starts patterns of current in the optic nerve fibers. The nerve currents from the two eyes travel up the optic nerve to a center in the midbrain where the impulses from the corresponding parts of the two eyes are combined to achieve psychological fusion. These impulses are then carried to the cerebral cortex, with patterns of excitation spreading to the occipital, parietal, and temporal lobes. Then, by some mysterious process, the letters and letter order configurations are perceived as a word and, later, word sequences as shown in the following diagram.

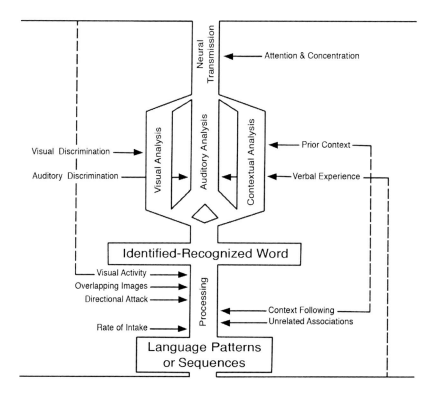

Neural Transmission

The intensity of the neural impressions[1] that will determine the vividness and clarity of word impressions is directly proportional to the **attention** and **concentration** capabilities of the reader.

In this regard, there appear to be two principal factors to be considered. One is the ability of the reader to focus his or her attention: to direct attention to the task at hand and to reduce the number and variety of extraneous excitations that could cause distraction and/or diversion of attention, thereby increasing the acceptance of the excitations from the current stimulus. Research studies suggest that individuals vary considerably in their ability to focus their attention and their ability to overcome distraction. It would appear that ability to focus attention is in large measure an acquired behavior pattern. Mirsky (1999) stated that "attention represents a highly articulated form of consciousness that has been shaped and modified by learning and experience."

The second factor is the reader's ability to concentrate or to sustain a level of attention that enables him or her to maintain a high level of interaction with the reading content. The considerations that determine the reader's level of attention are his or her attitudes concerning reading, motivation in a specific reading situation, and the level of physical comfort experienced while carrying out the reading task.

Too often, lack of attention or inability to concentrate is ascribed to lack of ability or to inadequate motivation. In the author's opinion, a reader's attention and concentration are more directly influenced by his or her general visual/functional competence, mental well-being, and the acquired attitudes that result from his or her reading successes or failures, in addition to the extent to which he or she has learned to focus attention and sustain concentration.

The Word as Our Fundamental Unit of Recognition

When examining the process of identification and recognition in reading, one must quickly conclude that the word is our smallest unit of visual identification and meaningful recognition. While we can identify and recognize letters, these do not convey or communicate meaning. Words, on the other hand, do suggest meaning, sometimes many meanings. Thus, we are concerned with words not as conveyors of absolute meaning or concepts, but

---

1. Titchener (1908) uses the term "attensity" to describe the clearness, vividness, prominence, or insistence of neural impressions.

rather as building blocks of concepts and communication.

One sometimes hears reference to the phrase as being a recognition unit. This assumption is completely refuted by hundreds of eye-movement photography studies and by other studies, such as that of Feinberg (1949), and Legge, Cheung, Yu, Chung, Lee, and Owens (2007), which explained, in part, the physiological basis for the relatively small span of recognition employed by most readers.

Nor can we accept the phrase as an absolute unit of recognition linguistically, for it is meaningful only in light of the sentence in which it functions. Except in isolated and limited instances, the phrase cannot be regarded as an independent thought unit. This position is further substantiated by a study by Koehler (1960), which suggested that the manner in which a reader relates one word to another is a highly individual matter.

Reading, then, must be considered initially as a word gathering process that provides the mind with the means for realizing phrases or similar linguistic sequences, which are ultimately combined in order to discern meaning and to stimulate elaborative thought. Kim, Knox, and Brown (2007) and Wagner (1999) stated that words are visually processed ahead of cognitive processes that later confirm word recognition and association in the realization of phrases and other long-term syntactical information. While no one can say with certainty exactly how words are isolated, identified, and recognized,[2] there appear to be three different avenues of comprehension that can be used separately but are often used in combination: visual analysis, auditory analysis, and the reader's knowledge and experience with the meaning and use of the word.

Visual Analysis

First, consider the area of visual analysis. A number of researchers have studied the structural or graphic aspects of words in an attempt to discover the factors that are most significant in effecting word recognition. The following examples show some of the factors that have been isolated.

---

2. Identification of words relates to the stage of becoming aware of all of their graphic characteristics. Recognition is the stage during which the reader associates the word form with meaning or sound. A reader can demonstrate the ability to identify a word from a foreign language by duplicating or matching it but still not be able to recognize the word in terms of meaning or sound. For recognition to take place, a word must be known.

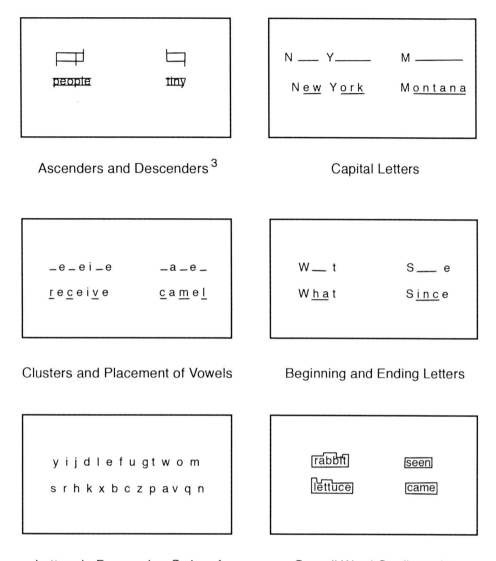

Ascenders and Descenders[3]

Capital Letters

Clusters and Placement of Vowels

Beginning and Ending Letters

Letters in Decreasing Order of
Ease of Identification[4]

Overall Word Configuration

Word Parts–Readers react to word structure, noting prefixes, suffixes, and other pronounceable parts. Wilkins (1917) presented scrambled words such as "Woodson Wilrow" (as seen in the following examples) and noted the tendency of students to recognize them as familiar words, i.e., "Woodrow

---

3. The parts of letters that project above and below the word shape are aids to recognition.
4. From a study by Crosland and Johnson (1928).

Wilson," indicating the tendency of people to use letter configurations as a means of word identification. This study also pointed out the inaccuracy that can occur as a result of too gross or superficial a reaction to letters, letter order configuration, and certain word characteristics.

Woodson Wilrow

talder powcum

Psychment Departology

Fronts and Backs of Words—In a study by Huey (1898), readers were presented with two selections, the first consisting of only the beginning of words and the second consisting of only the last half of words, as seen in the following display. This first selection was read by adult subjects at an average rate of 29 words per minute, and the second selection was read at an average rate of 20 words per minute. The fact that both rates were so significantly lower than usual reading rates for adults (150–155 wpm) suggested that the total word configuration is essential for successful word identification and recognition.

The	conch	we	establ	eai	i
19	Il you	doc	n na	reac	tr
culmi	o	yea	o stu	ar	investi
Ho	exac	we	hi find	t b	inter
w,	tly,	re	is	ings o e	pre-
ted ?	n ms f	sic	nan	ire,	at d
ey	an ?	ie st	or an	wer d	m o
sult	ie	ations	f	ers,	s t id

Tops and Bottoms of Words—There is little doubt that the first selection is easier to read than the second because of a difference in the amount of letter cues provided. Following, is an example of how the tops of letters furnish more cues than do the bottoms.

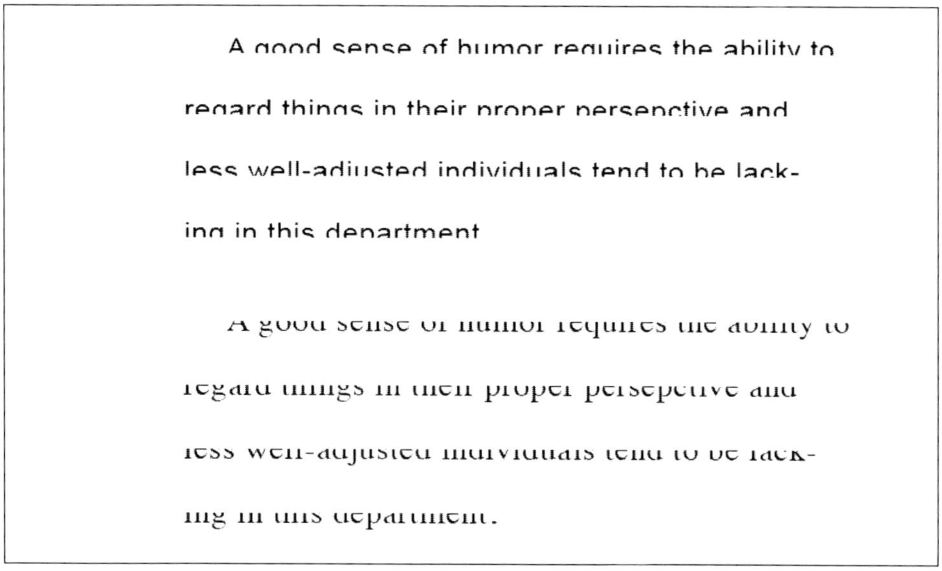

A good sense of humor requires the ability to

regard things in their proper perspective and

less well-adjusted individuals tend to be lack-

ing in this department

A good sense of humor requires the ability to

regard things in their proper perspective and

less well-adjusted individuals tend to be lack-

ing in this department.

Interior White Spaces–Note in the following display that the top line is more easily readable than the lower line because of the presence of interior space within the letters, which is as critical to letter recognition as the outer contour.

HOW DICKDOCKETS DICK DOCKETS

author of treasure hunting

author of treasure hunting

Typefaces–Some typefaces facilitate recognition, while others hinder the process by employing less familiar and/or less distinguishable letterforms, as seen in the following samples.

Right to Read
Right to Read
Right to Read

Letter Sequence—Each word has left-to-right and top-to-bottom spatial orientation that is critical to its recognition. A simple inversion of a line of print or a reversal of the letter order illustrates how dependent one is on the spatial orientation of each word, as shown in the following examples.

teacher will find it adventageous to use the instrument with

the entire class using very easy material so that most

students will be able to read with good comprehension.

One can only conclude, after considering all the means by which a word can be apprehended visually, that the reader reacts initially to the total word through an awareness of the grid or pattern of retinal stimulation caused by the light reflected from the printed page through and around the letters of that word. One's eyes are stimulated in much the same fashion as a photo-electric cell, processing a total letter impression that might look like that which is depicted in the following illustration.

Only when this has been done can the reader react to letter cues, the spatial orientation of letters, and the word's individual shape. Following this, the reader employs one or more of the means of visual analysis previously described in order to recognize the word. In essence, then, the reader can use these visual analysis cues for word recognition only after he or she has reacted to the total word pattern.

Although the initial reaction is to the total letter configuration of a word, the reader is seldom aware of this reaction (unless he or she is a beginning reader or is identifying less familiar or unfamiliar words), for most visual analysis is carried on as a subliminal activity. During the relatively high-speed process of reading, three (in the case of beginning readers) to five (in the case of advanced readers) impressions per second are being fed to the mind. While some words may be recognized on the instant of contact, it would seem logical to assume that many words are first simply identified as letter constructs, and then stored in short-term memory to be recalled and recognized slightly later, in conjunction with the suggestions of the context.

The reader's competence in identifying and recognizing words will be directly influenced by his or her acquired orthographic competency or the learned ability to visually discriminate letters, letter order, and word forms. Discrimination is also dependent on the reader's ability to concentrate sufficient attention on a word in order to apprehend all of the visual cues that are available. Students vary considerably in this capability. In fact, some children judged to be good readers are poor spellers because of a lack of adequate visual discrimination ability, but read well by virtue of a higher level of intelligence and a more extensive verbal background that later allows words to be recognized in light of the content in which they appear, or perhaps they are bypassed.

Auditory Analysis

The second major avenue of word recognition is auditory analysis. Generally, a reader of any age will have experienced a great quantity of words as auditory sound sequences prior to encountering them in printed form (exceptions to this will be specific proper nouns, technical words, and other words of a low-frequency nature). Thus, a reader's ability to identify clusters of letters, which may constitute words or parts of words as sound units, assists him or her in recognizing words. It should be mentioned, however, that this form of recognition is a somewhat slower and more conscious process than visual analysis. Auditory analysis is initiated by visual analysis, during which the reader identifies a particular group of letters and realizes that group as a unit of sound. In addition, it should be noted that a reader employing audi-

tory analysis usually departs from a regular or fluent reading process to accomplish this process. Seldom can conscious auditory analysis be employed
without a pronounced change in eye-movement behavior in the form of
additional fixations or regressions.

Even if auditory background serves to help students' anticipation of
words in content to be encountered, it is unlikely that phonological awareness serves word recognition initially. Frost (1998) proposed this in his min-
imality principle, which states that readers recognize words using minimal
phonological realization to access a unique lexical entry. According to this
principle, "Skilled readers do not represent prosodic information en route to
word recognition, but may activate full phonological representations after
lexical access."

When a child starts learning to read, he or she has a vast auditory stockpile of words and experiences. The child needs to learn only to isolate and
distinguish portions of these auditory experiences and relate these to their
printed counterparts in order to "read" many words. Whether a phonetic or
nonphonetic approach is used to teach reading, a child will, in varying degrees and in individual ways, learn to associate letters and letter groups with
sound equivalents. The extent to which the child can do this is dependent on
acquired auditory discrimination ability and how well he or she is taught to
associate graphemes with phonemes.

It is sometimes mistakenly supposed that a child hears all the sounds that
comprise a word and realizes the sequence of sounds in a word as he or she
speaks it. There is accumulating evidence, however, to indicate that this may
not be the case and that many children monitor their speech kinesthetically
with a low degree of auditory discrimination. It seems apparent that a reader cannot associate specific sounds with letters or letter configurations unless
he or she has first truly heard those specific sounds and isolated them as pronounceable entities.

Thus, the degree to which a reader can employ auditory analysis to decode words will depend, to a great extent, on his or her verbal experience,
acquired auditory discrimination ability, skill in phonetic analysis, acquired
visual discrimination ability, and proficiency in contextual analysis.

It should be mentioned at this point that the major function of auditory
analysis or decoding should be to introduce printed words to the mind so
that, in subsequent encounters, visual analysis can predominate, permitting
more direct and rapid identification and recognition. Auditory analysis
should be regarded as helpful and desirable when employed consciously as
a means of unlocking unfamiliar words and for the way it helps the reader to
inspect a word or word parts more minutely. However, if a reader begins to
depend on auditory analysis excessively, the tendency to translate words into

their sound equivalents and/or speech movements (as is the case with readers who vocalize), inhibition of the reading process will ultimately occur and real fluency in reading will never be realized (Woodworth, 1938). Goodman and Niles (1970) used the term "recoding" to describe the translation of print into sound as an assist to deriving meaning. They stated that, at best, recoding plays a supplemental role. According to Goodman and Niles (1970), "When silent reading becomes proficient, it becomes a very different process from oral reading. It is much more rapid and not tied to encoding what is being read as speech."

Contextual Analysis

A third avenue of recognition is contextual analysis. Use of this path of word recognition is, of course, highly dependent on the reader's ability to use context clues to aid in comprehension, which is, in turn, dependent on his or her experiential background. Goodman and Niles (1970) referred to this capability as the reader's ability to use syntactic information (sentence patterns, pattern markers, and transformational rules) as well as semantic information (experience, concepts, and vocabulary).

The reader's use of context and meaning, however, is always preceded by visual analysis. The amount of visual analysis required is directly dependent on the linguistic probability of the occurrence of certain words in the context and the reader's ability to use context clues to predict the occurrence of certain words. Less familiar words and unexpected words require the greatest amount of conscious visual monitoring on the part of the reader if he or she is to maintain complete accuracy in recognition and reading. More familiar words and those that immediately suggest themselves as a means of completing the author's thought require the least conscious monitoring.

In those instances in which the context suggests no specific word or too many word possibilities, the reader must attend to the visual characteristics of words to maintain accuracy. This is likewise true in those instances in which the context suggests one word to the reader and then employs a different word.

In these latter conditions, visual analysis must provide the basis for correcting the perceptual process, or inaccurate recognition and misunderstanding will undoubtedly occur.

To illustrate the interdependence of context clues and visual analysis, the selection shown in the following paragraph has been presented to many audiences.

Before   skin   diving   became   ___(1)___ , sharks   were   highly ___(2)___ . The sight of a ___(3)___ fin ___(4)___ the water struck fear in the heart of the ___(5)___ . Then a new ___(6)___ emerged, donning equipment called ___(7)___ .

The audience members were asked to call out the words they felt were appropriate for the blanks. Certain blanks elicited immediate responses. Others required prolonged pondering before a word was supplied. Still other blanks suggested no words at all.

In the examples shown on the following page, see the typical responses of thousands of adults viewing this paragraph. The first column lists their responses with no visual clues; the second and third columns show responses when visual clues were progressively added.

It is apparent that the number of letter clues required for word recognition varies with the probability of a given word occurring in the content and the degree to which words are familiar. It is also evident that once a word has been selected by a reader, he or she tends to persist in the choice of that word until it is confirmed or invalidated by a visual analysis. As a result of this exercise, in which all words were known words, it becomes evident that the content implies the presence of certain words, and visual analysis confirms or rejects the words suggested.

In contemplating the manner in which contextual analysis and visual analysis interact during the very dynamic process of reading, it is important to realize that the reader averages three to five fixations per second. At this high input rate, it is not possible for the reader to become involved in prolonged word inspection or deliberation over the possibilities of content without conscious and noticeable deviation from the process of fluent silent reading. Either a word will instantly suggest itself and be recognized upon contact, or the word will be identified and stored in short-term memory to be recalled later as other words are identified and recognized. In other words, a reader uses prior context as well as subsequent content to recognize a word.

Weaver (1963) substantiated the use of bilateral context clues. He stated that the five words preceding a word and the five following words yield the most significant contextual clues for a particular word. It would seem that a reader, in most cases, uses context to anticipate the author's trend of thought and verbal expression, but in many cases must delay confirmation of a specific word until he or she has passed it, some .75 seconds to 1.5 seconds later

WORD #	WITH NO CUES	WITH FIRST AND LAST LETTER	WITH FIRST, SECOND and LAST LETTER
1.	Rapidly and almost unanimously, *popular* is selected.	p____r *Popular* is immediately reinforced.	po___r *Popular* seems quite definite.
2.	*Feared* is usually selected, but after a certain amount of deliberation, indicating a searching through of probabilities. Sometimes an illogical word, such as "prized" or "scarce" is suggested, showing a certain disregard of content.	f____d *Feared* is now confirmed, unanimously and immediately.	fe____d *Feared* is still confirmed.
3.	*Dorsal* is selected only occasionally and by people with more experience with fish. The more common choices, and those more probable, are "triangular" and "black."	d____l If *dorsal* had been mentioned, this is immediately reinforced.	do___l *Dorsal* is now confirmed.
4.	Numerous choices are made rather quickly: "splitting," "slicing," "skimming," and "cut-	s____g "Cutting" is now ruled out, but the other choices still hold.	sp___g Hesitantly, the final selection of *splitting* is usually made at this point.
5.	There is usually a long delay in the contemplation of this word. Then a few tentative choices will be made: "swimmer," "diver," "fisherman," and "bather."	b____r "Bather" is now the only choice that is suggested.	be___r Now even "bather" is ruled out. Usually no logical word is selected. Sometimes "believer" and "beginner" are selected. Almost no one guesses the correct choice—*beholder*.
6.	Many times there is no response to this word at all.	c___t After a great deal of deliberation, *cult* may be suggested by a few.	cu__t *Cult* now is confirmed.
7.	Those who are familiar with skin diving will hesitantly mention *SCUBA*. The rest will make no attempt to select a word.	S___A *SCUBA* is confirmed, if it has been mentioned. If it has not yet been mentioned, it is usually guessed by many at this point.	SC_A *SCUBA* is definitely confirmed.

(three to five words) as previously cited by Kim, Knox, and Brown (2007), and Wagner (1999). This delayed confirmation process was quite evident when audiences reacted to the sample paragraph on skin diving. They would often supply a word and then withdraw it and suggest another possibility as they read more of a particular sentence.

In summary, it seems probable that a reader uses context (syntax) to anticipate both words and ideas, employs visual analysis upon the instant of contact with a word to effect identification and recognition or storage, sometimes deviates from reading to employ auditory analysis (recoding) to unlock and recognize less familiar words, and then uses the "context following" to confirm the accuracy of specific words selected. Recognition then must be thought of, for the most part, as a multifaceted process that typically lags behind visual intake.

Processing

Processing can be defined as a stage during which words are stored and sufficiently stabilized in a manner that will allow them to be retrieved along with other words and realized as language patterns or phrase sequences. The stage of processing is maintained as an ongoing activity concurrent with the process of word intake, but lagging slightly behind.

As a consequence of the dynamic nature of reading, there are various influences on a reader's ability to process words with competence. These influences are as follows: the kinesthesia or the muscular activity of the visual activity, the overlapping of retinal impressions, the sequence of impressions (resulting from the reader's directional attack), the influence of the context following a given word, the effect of unrelated associations, and the rate of the input of impressions.

Gilbert (1959a) conducted a study entitled, "Saccadic Movements as a Factor in Visual Perception in Reading," which substantiated the fact that visual impressions can deteriorate as a result of the kinesthesia of the visual activity.

In this study, two-word units were exposed tachistoscopically, as shown in the following manner, in rapid sequence in the same place on a projection screen so as to require no eye movements on the part of the reader. Retention of the material was checked.

Then, similar two-word groups were presented along a line on a projection screen, as shown in the following display, requiring the reader to make a series of eye movements in order to apprehend the material. Retention was again checked.

Our school   will have   open house   this year.

Results indicated that there was significantly less retention when eye movements were employed. Comparisons of the better readers (in the upper quartile) with the poorer readers (in the lowest quartile) indicated that the poorer readers retained substantially less when eye movements were required.

These results are not difficult to understand when one considers that poorer readers will generally have more difficulty with binocular coordination and fusion, and less motility (ease or facility in making ocular rotations).

Thus, it would appear that the amount that is retained from each visual impression is in direct proportion to the energy consumed by the physical act of moving the eyes along a line of print, and the quality of the visual discrimination that can be accomplished.

Another Gilbert (1959b) study, entitled "Speed of Processing Visual Stimuli and Its Relation to Reading," demonstrated the effect of overlapping images. In this study, Gilbert gave groups of students a series of tachistoscopic exposures in which one, two, three, four, and five words were flashed. Retention was checked. Then similar exposures were made and then immediately overlapped with nonsense material, as seen in the next example, causing aberration of the original word exposures.

Item 1

(1)   words
(b) hypytkoie

Item 2

(a)   his best shoes
(b) bnvcrmxztghjfedka

Item 3

(a)   they will come home early
(b) saqwsxcderfubgtyhjshuiklopzxc

Again, retention was checked. Then the amount of time between the initial exposure and the overlap was gradually prolonged, and retention was checked with each increased interval. Gilbert found that there was a substantial loss of the initial impression as a result of the superimposition of another impression. Further, the loss was greater when the number of words was greater (a more complex perceptual and organizational task). When the poorer readers were again compared with better readers, it was found that the poorer readers lost even more retention because of the overlapping images and also tended to require a greater interval of time between the word exposures and the overlapping nonsense material in order to satisfactorily stabilize, or process, their visual impressions.

The ramifications of this study, combined with Feinberg's findings (1949) and Legge, et al. (2007) regarding the fall-off of visual acuity, help to explain why the span of recognition is as small as it has been found to be. It is not possible to say with any degree of certainty how large the span of recognition is at the moment of initial contact with words, for immediately upon a shift of the reader's eyes, another retinal impression superimposes itself on the initial impression and this condition reduces the amount of the initial impression that can be salvaged or retained by the reader. Thus, the average span of recognition referred to in the process of eye-movement recording could be regarded as "salvageable" span. It is not difficult, then, to understand why poorer or less mature readers possess smaller spans of recognition and require longer intervals of duration of fixation to adequately process their impressions when one considers that their reduced discrimination skills will inhibit their ability to use orthographic impressions, and that their inadequate verbal skills will limit their ability to use context clues.

Thus, it is apparent that the overlap of images or retinal impressions lessens, in varying degrees, the accuracy with which words are processed by a reader.

Since salvageable span (average span of recognition) is comparatively limited, even for better readers, language patterns or phrasing can be realized only from a series of visual impressions and apprehensions. Therefore, directional attack, or the sequence of impressions, bears directly on the accuracy with which a reader recalls and comprehends. The following graphs portray the inherently greater reorganizational task that faces the poorer reader who regresses more frequently, and yet, who is less qualified for the task of reorganizing word impressions than the more accomplished reader. The student whose graph is shown on the left is an efficient reader with an orderly directional attack. The graph on the right shows an inefficient reader with a poor directional attack. Looking at the manner in which both readers move across a line of print, one can imagine the amount of confusion experienced by the poor reader as well as the greater need to reorganize content in order to comprehend accurately.

In studies by Buswell (1922), E. A. Taylor (1937 and 1959), Gilbert (1953); and S. E. Taylor, Frackenpohl, and Pettee (1959), one finds a direct relationship between academic achievement and directional attack difficulty (the percentage of regressive fixations to forward fixations). Further, it is the author's experience that there exists a direct relationship between directional attack and reading comprehension, which undoubtedly results from the sequence, accuracy, and rate of input of words into short-term memory from which a reader later recalls to utilize word impressions.

A reader will likely in .75 to 1.5 seconds, following visual contact with a particular word, confirm his or her original impression of that word by virtue of the context following the word as cited by Kim, Knox, and Brown (2007). A reader will constantly confirm or alter the original word impression as he or she retrieves or recalls impressions of the words that are read. Thus, a reader's ability to retrieve impressions with accuracy is dependent on his or her ability to associate those later word impressions with the author's message and train of thought.

Beyond the direct or more meaningful associations a reader has with the words he or she encounters, there are numerous other unrelated associations that can either reinforce or deteriorate the original word impressions. Sometimes a reader will be affected by factors completely unrelated to the meaning of the sentence in which they appear. For instance, a student may respond more strongly to one word because of difficulty he or she had in learning to spell it, or he or she will associate another word with a joke or a party game. Still other words may evoke emotional responses, calling forth either negative or positive reactions. These irrelevant reactions to words can at times also alter the effectiveness and accuracy with which a reader recognizes and retains the words as originally encountered in context.

Still another factor to be considered in the process of fluent silent reading is the rate of word intake. Characteristically, a reader will observe a rate of reading that permits adequate time for assimilation of words and ideas. His or her characteristic duration of fixation and the amount of fixations employed during reading reflect this perceptual requirement. Not all readers, however, make this adjustment. The readers who do not are those who tolerate superficial understanding of what they read and achieve less than satisfactory comprehension. This condition often occurs with readers whose visual problems result in ocular discomfort, which prompts them to progress more rapidly than they should through reading material in order to get the task "over with."

When one considers that most readers employ a rather involuntary oculomotor activity in silent reading, and that this activity usually is quite habitual in the case of less capable readers regardless of variations in content, one can appreciate the perceptual handicap of the less capable reader who frequently finds that he or she has too little time to adequately process word impressions and as a consequence, becomes conditioned to make additional fixations over a word, regress frequently, or reread entire portions of a selection.

The significance of this situation can be further appreciated when considering the results of a study by S. E. Taylor and H. A. Robinson (1963) in which it was shown that a beginning reader's pause time seemed not to be governed by his or her word identification and recognition requirements, but rather by the motivation of his or her habitual ocular performance.

What happens when reading time is limited and a reader tries to accelerate beyond his or her usual rate of efficient intake? A reader who possesses a visual-functional and perceptual reserve will be able to alert himself or herself to a "higher than usual" attention level and likewise will be able to expend the energy needed to maintain an "accelerated reading rate." Such a reader will be able to increase his or her reading rate without sacrificing accuracy and comprehension.

For the reader who does not possess this reserve, physical demands may cause discomfort and the multitude of impressions and the abbreviated processing time can cause a "recognition overload." As a result, this reader will find himself or herself forced to reread more frequently in order to maintain perceptual accuracy and adequate comprehension. Often this "rechecking" time will prevent him or her from achieving the desired higher rate, with a possible lessening of retention and comprehension.

In the reading field, there has long been the feeling that the faster a reader reads, the better he or she comprehends. It is the author's conviction that this is the case only when the reader's ability to function visually and perceptually is adequate, and the ability to associate is "up to the task of accelerated reading" that he or she will be able to benefit from this increased intake per minute.

Fortunately, today there are quite sophisticated, yet easy-to-use eye-movement recording techniques that can assist in evaluating a student's efficiency in the visual, perceptual, and information processing skills that the author terms the Fundamental Reading Process. These techniques will be described in Chapter 2.

Then in Chapters 4, 5, and 6 there will be a further examination of the factors and influences that impinge on a student's ability to become a truly fluent silent reader and how today's computer training techniques can improve the 30 or more subliminal functions employed in reading that will lead to more meaningful proficiency and fluency in silent reading.

Language Patterns or Sequences of Information

As each word is processed, it is added to and becomes part of the larger message that is recognized in the form of language patterns. Now the reader will understand or react to an ever-growing and accumulating message of the selection being read.

UNDERSTANDING AND/OR REACTING

In this phase, the reader brings into play all of his or her experience and background and employs a multitude of mental organizational processes, as depicted in the following diagram, that allow him or her, either sequentially or simultaneously, to index information, make comparisons, note sequence, react by forming sensory impressions, or appreciate what is being conveyed or the manner in which it is conveyed. These processes are often a combination of cognitive and affective reactions.

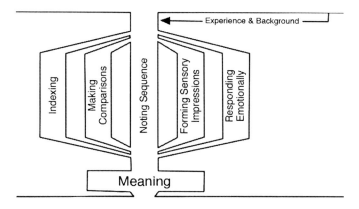

It is of interest to note that the manner by which a person understands and reads is quite similar to that employed during listening, as stated by S. E. Taylor (1964). For this reason, reading and listening measurements have always correlated highly.

Indexing

In indexing, the reader assigns relative values to bits of information. He or she looks for main ideas and supporting details, separates the relevant from the irrelevant, and, in other ways, creates a sort of mental outline by ranking the information according to importance. For example, in reading an article on safety at school, a student might note those hazards that are most serious and then file away under each type of accident the different ways in which it would occur, its frequency of occurrence, and means of prevention. Some students who are exceptionally skilled in mental indexing report the ability to visualize an outline as they read.

Making Comparisons

In making comparisons, the reader notes similarities and differences. This allows him or her to learn about something new and relate it to something already known or see additional relationships by categorizing information. For example, a common application of this approach would occur in reading about a foreign country, for an author frequently relates the climate, population, natural resources, and social customs of the unknown country to an area familiar to the reader. When this comparison is not made by the author, some students will often make such comparisons on their own in order to aid their comprehension.

Noting Sequence

In noting sequence, the reader arranges the material according to time, space, position, degree, or some other relationship. It is easier to remember a description of a journey if one arranges the places in the order in which they were visited, visualizes the distance traveled, or remembers the order of the events that occurred during each stage of the trip. All of these approaches aid the reader in creating a larger structure or framework into which bits of information can be placed, thus aiding retention and making possible maximum utilization of the information.

Forming Sensory Impressions

In forming sensory impressions, the reader reacts with his or her senses—taste, touch, smell, sight, and hearing. Of these five sensory responses, the one most frequently called upon is sight, or the ability to visualize. Readers who are highly skilled in forming sensory impressions also find it possible to taste tastes, smell smells, and translate words into other types of sensory impressions.

Responding Emotionally

Readers also respond emotionally to people, situations, and events. These reactions are initiated by the reader's attitude and behavior, personal values and goals, and the social mores of his or her peer group, community, and the society of which he or she is a part. Oftentimes, an emotional reaction can be sufficiently strong to distort the literal or objective meaning of the message, so, in essence, this reaction could at times have the effect of either adding to the meaning of the content or detracting from it.

Elaborative and/or Divergent Thinking

After the reader has comprehended the meaning or reacted to the content of the material, he or she may advance to another stage, one of elaborative and divergent thinking. At various intervals during the reading or after having understood and reacted to substantial portions of the content, the reader may become involved in evaluation, interpretation, application, and appreciation, as shown in the following diagram.

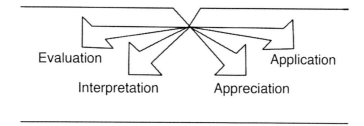

During this stage, the reader evaluates what has been read, recognizing whether the events are natural or implausible developments, whether the characters are real or stereotyped, and whether the tone is sincere or artificial. He or she proceeds to make additional associations and interpretations, relating what was read to his or her own experiences, convictions, and interests. The reader might appreciate the aesthetic content and form of a message, as he or she pauses to reflect on the quality and nature of the reading material that was experienced. The reader may also apply what was read, taking action, for example, by writing a letter to a local legislator. Apart from reading, a reader may alter his or her manner of speaking or acting, having identified with a fictional character or become aware of an objectionable personal trait. The reader may add to a stockpile of mental content and become a more interesting conversationalist, or perhaps he or she will become a better-informed citizen who acts more intelligently and with greater capability.

CONCLUSION

From the time the light from the printed page strikes the reader's eyes until he or she has assimilated the message, the reader has been involved in about 30 different processes of seeing, perceiving, understanding, and reacting. The fact that these processes are cyclical in nature and impinge so closely upon one another makes it difficult for teachers of reading to isolate them, either for purposes of measurement and evaluation, or in order to provide improved and appropriate instruction. It is essential, however, for teachers to be aware of the multifaceted nature of the reading process, and to understand the sequence and relationship of the various steps in selecting and using reading improvement techniques.

Over the years, most reading development programs have concentrated on the latter stages of the reading process, with little, if any, attention to the skills involved in the seeing and perceiving stages that initiate reading. It is encouraging to note that more and more reading specialists are becoming aware of the need for training in these areas and are taking steps to provide it. Fortunately, more refined techniques and computer programs are becoming available for such silent reading practice, and these more sophisticated instructional systems do include specific training in seeing and perception as part of a comprehensive program of reading development. Also, more and more schools are realizing the need to provide such forms of instruction, and an increasing number of teacher training institutions are providing the kind of professional training that will help teachers to make competent use of the new methods and materials.

It is hoped that this model of the reading process will contribute toward the goal of all who are concerned with reading: to make possible more comprehensive and efficient instruction that results in the development of competent, thoughtful, lifetime readers.

QUESTIONS THAT COULD ARISE
AFTER READING THIS CHAPTER

1. What are the unseen, unheard skills involved in silent reading fluency that are not treated in most reading programs today?
2. Why is the development of the visual and perceptual skills of reading not considered in most core reading programs?
3. How can one detect students with limited perceptual capability?
4. How many students experience vision and visual/functional difficulties and how could these difficulties be detected in school screenings?
5. In what way can today's computer technology be employed to improve many of the factors or processes of reading that are required for meaningful fluency in silent reading to be attained?

REFERENCES

Bartiss, M. (2005). *Extraocular muscles: Convergence insufficiency.* eMedicine.com, Inc., eMedicine Specialties, Ophthalmology.

Bing, L. B. (1964). Vision readiness and reading readiness. In J. Allen Figurel (Ed.), *Improvement of reading through classroom practice, 9* (pp. 268–271). International Reading Association Conference Proceedings.

Buckingham, B. R. (1931). *New data on the typography of textbooks.* Yearbook of the National Society for the Study of Education, 9–125.

Buswell, G. T. (1922). Fundamental reading habits: A study of their development. *Supplementary Educational Monographs No 21,* xiv, 150.

Convergence Insufficiency Treatment Trial Study Group 2. (2008). Randomized clinical trial of treatments for symptomatic convergence insufficiency in children. *Archives of Ophthalmology, 126*(10), 1336–1349.

Crosland, H. R., & Johnson, G. (1928). The range of apprehension as affected by inter-letter hair-spacing and by the characteristics of individual letters. *Journal of Applied Psychology, 12*(1), 82–124.

Eames, T. H. (1932). A comparison of the ocular characteristics of unselected and reading disability groups. *Journal of Educational Research, 24,* 211–215.

Feinberg, R. (1949). A study of some aspects of peripheral visual acuity. *American Journal of Optometry and Archives of American Academy of Optometrics, 26,* 49–56.

Frost, R. (1998). Towards a strong phonological theory of visual word recognition: True issues and false trails. *Psychological Bulletin 123,* 71–99.

Gilbert, L. C. (1953). Functional motor efficiency of the eyes and its relation to reading. *University of California Publications in Education, 3,* 159–231.

Gilbert, L. C. (1959a). Saccadic movements as a factor in visual perception in reading. *Journal of Educational Psychology, 50*(1), 15–19.

Gilbert, L. C. (1959b). Speed of processing visual stimuli and its relation to reading. *Journal of Educational Psychology, 50,* 8–14.

Good, G. H. (1939). Relationship of fusion weakness to reading disability. *Journal of Experimental Education, 8,* 115–121.

Goodman, K. S., & Niles, O. S. (1970). *Reading: Process and program.* Champaign, Illinois: National Council of Teachers of English, Quotations from Behind the Eye: What Happens in Reading, 3–38.

Gould, L. N., Henderson, E., & Scheele, R. L. (1964). Vision motor perception program in the Brentwood public schools. In J. Allen Figurel (Ed.), *Improvement of reading through classroom practice, 9* (pp. 271–276). International Reading Association Conference Proceedings.

Huey, E. B. (1898). Preliminary experiments in the physiology and psychology of reading. *American Journal of Psychology, 9,* 575–586.

Imus, H. A., Rothney, J. W. M., & Baer, R. U. (1938). *An evaluation of visual factors in reading.* Hanover, New Hampshire: Dartmouth College Publications.

Kephart, N. C. (1960). *The slow learner in the classroom.* Columbus, Ohio: Charles E. Merrill.

Kim, K., Knox, M., & Brown, J. (2007). Eye movement and strategic reading. In Y. Goodman & P. Martens (Eds.), *Critical issues in early literacy: Research and pedagogy* (pp. 47–58). New Jersey: Lawrence Erlbaum Associates, Inc.

Koehler, W. B. (1960). Phrased reading: Final report. *Independent School Bulletin, 60–61,* 14–18.

Legge, G. E., Cheung, S.-H., Yu, D., Chung, S. T. L., Lee, H.-W., & Owens, D. P. (2007). The case for the visual span as a sensory bottleneck in reading. *Journal of Vision, 7*(2):9, 1–15.

Luckiesh, M., & Moss, F. K. (1941). Visuality and readability of print on white and tinted papers. *Journal of Applied Psychology, 25,* 152–158.

Mirsky, A. F. (1999). Disorders of attention: A neuropsychological perspective. In G. R. Lyon & N. A. Krasnegor (Eds.), *Attention, memory, and executive function* (2nd printing, pp. 71–96). Baltimore: Paul H. Brookes Publishing Co.

Robinson, H. M. (1958). The findings of research on visual difficulties and reading. *Reading for Effective Living, 3,* 107–111. International Reading Association Conference Proceedings.

Robinson, H. M., & Huelsman, Jr., C. B. (1952). Visual efficiency and progress in learning to read. *Clinical Studies in Reading, II, Supplementary Educational Monographs, No. 77,* 31–63.

Scheiman, M., Mitchell, G. L., Cotter, S., Cooper, J., Kulp, M., Rouse, M., Borsting, E., London, R., & Wensveen, J. (2005). A randomized clinical trial of treatments for convergence insufficiency in children. *Archives of Ophthalmology, 123,* 14–24.

Taylor, E. A. (1937). *Controlled reading.* Chicago, Illinois: University of Chicago Press.

Taylor, E. A. (1959). *Eyes, visual anomalies, and the fundamental reading skill.* New York: Reading and Study Skills Center.

Taylor, E. A. (1966). *The fundamental reading skill* (2nd ed.), xviii, 157. Springfield, Illinois: Charles C Thomas.

Taylor, S. E. (1964). *Listening. What research says to the teacher, 29.* Washington, DC: National Education Association.

Taylor, S. E. (1965). The relationship of the oculomotor efficiency of the beginning reader to success in learning to read. *Research and Information Bulletin No. 6.* Huntington, New York: Educational Developmental Laboratories, Inc.

Taylor, S. E. (1995). *Visagraph® resource guide.* Huntington Station, New York: Instructional Communications, Inc.

Taylor, S. E., Frackenpohl, H., & Pettee, J. L. (1959). A report on two studies of the validity of eye-movement photography as a measurement of reading performance. *Reading in a Changing Society, 2,* 240–245. International Reading Association Conference Proceedings. Also available as EDL Research and Information Bulletin No. 2. Huntington, New York: Educational Developmental Laboratories, Inc.

Taylor, S. E., & Robinson, H. A. (1963). The relationship of the oculomotor efficiency of the beginning reader to his success in learning to read. A paper presented at the American Educational Research Association Conference.

Tinker, M. A. (1963). *Legibility of print,* 236–246. Ames, Iowa: Iowa State University Press.

Titchener, E. B. (1908). Lectures on the elementary psychology of feeling and attention.

Wagner, R. K. (1999). From simple structure to complex function: Major trends in the development of theories, models, and measurements of memory. In G. R. Lyon & N. A. Krasnegor (Eds.), *Attention, memory, and executive function* (2nd printing, pp. 139–156). Baltimore: Paul H. Brookes.

Weaver, W. W. (1963). *The effect of direction of content on word predictability. New developments in programs and procedures for college-adult reading.* Twelfth yearbook of the National Reading Conference, 153–157.

Wilkins, M. C. (1917). A tachistoscopic experiment in reading. Unpublished master's thesis, Columbia University, 24.

Woodworth, R. S. (1938). *Experimental psychology,* 717–719. New York: Henry Holt & Company.

Chapter 2

EYE-MOVEMENT RECORDING
OF THE READING PROCESS

Stanford E. Taylor

This chapter will discuss how eye-movement recording can be used to assess the efficiency of the seeing, perceiving, and literal understanding processes involved in reading as described in Chapter 1. While there are many eye-movement recording devices used for research purposes that record very minute eye movements that include vertical movements, these devices are far more complex in operation and so are beyond what can or need to be used by a school to assess fluency in silent reading. Further, these research eye-movement recording devices do not auto-analyze data or relate this data to any reading norms.

The Visagraph® eye-movement recording system, developed by the author and referred to in Chapter 1 will be further described in this chapter. The Visagraph® is unique in that it automatically analyzes a resulting eye-movement recording in terms of national grade level norm performances as established by Taylor, Frackenpohl, and Pettee (1960). Eye-movement research recording devices do not auto analyze data or relate this data to reading norms. Further, the Visagraph® is the most widely used eye-movement recording system today (employed in thousands of schools). Although considerable detailed information is provided, the primary goal of this chapter is to simply acquaint the reader with the use of eye-movement recording to appraise what the author terms the Fundamental Reading Process, visual/functional proficiency, perceptual accuracy, and information processing competence, referred to in Chapter 1 as seeing and perceiving. Eye movement information regarding a student's efficiency or fluency in silent reading when combined with standardized or state tests, which measure a student's effectiveness, can provide a more complete evaluation of a reader's true proficiency in reading.

There is no more definitive means of evaluating a reader's fluency or efficiency in silent reading than administering an eye-movement recording. Silent reading rate and resulting comprehension may be used as general gauges of reading efficiency. However, what composes a reader's process, or exactly "how" he or she reads dynamically, can only be determined through eye-movement recording.

This chapter will only describe Visagraph® procedures with reading text selections, however, it should be noted that there are eye-movement recording tests available for very beginning nonreaders and more extensive testing methods for the examination of visual functional deficiencies.

While it would be desirable to administer an eye-movement recording with all students at different grade levels as they advance through their academic careers, this is not likely to be possible because of time constraints. However, eye-movement recordings should be administered with struggling or underachieving readers to determine whether a visual examination by a vision specialist is warranted, and to what extent fluency development techniques should be employed.

Let's examine the process of recording eye movements with a Visagraph® eye-movement recording system as seen in the following image. Today, this system is the easiest and quickest (five to seven minutes) means of recording and interpreting the process of silent reading.

RECORDING WITH THE VISAGRAPH®

When administering a Visagraph® recording, a student is given a reading selection appropriate for his or her reading level, typically on an independent reading level or slightly lower. The student puts on the Visagraph® goggles and the examiner adjusts the interpupilary setting (IPD) to ensure that the infrared sensors in the goggles are in proper alignment with the student's eyes. The subject is then instructed to read carefully for good comprehension, not rate. Then the recording begins as shown in the following picture. When the recording is completed, the student is asked 10 comprehension questions. A comprehension score of 70 percent or higher is deemed sufficient qualification to judge that the recording is most likely typical of the reader's silent reading performance. If the comprehension is less than 70 percent, it is recommended that another recording be made, perhaps one level lower than the original recording.

INTERPRETING READING RECORDINGS

After a reading recording is generated, four types of data presentations are available.

- **Reading Report**–presents the data as analyzed by the Visagraph® program in relation to national norms.
- **Simulation**–a display of the student's eyes moving across the text that was read.
- **Visual Functional Report**–presents data that relates to the ability of the student to use good or poor binocular coordination.
- **Graphs**–displays plots of the actual movement of the subject's eyes while reading.

Interpreting the Reading Report

The Reading Report, shown in the image that follows, provides the automatic calculations of all reading performance characteristics as well as a plot (graph) of these performances in relation to norms established by Taylor, Frackenpohl, and Pettee (1960). The information shown on the report can be used as a basis for reaching judgments about the subject's need for fluency development training, as will be discussed later in this book.

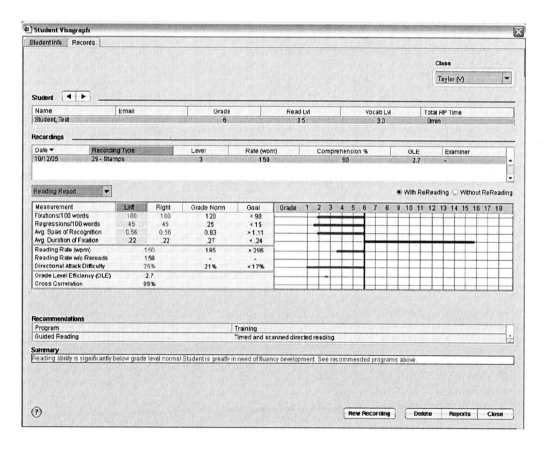

Automatic calculations of reading performance characteristics will appear as well as Grade Level Normative performances. In addition, there will be a plot of the characteristics of the most active eye against Taylor National Norms. Note that the shaded area in the report indicates the most active eye, not necessarily the dominant eye.

As one reviews a student's Reading Report, the following factors should be considered:

Fixations

The number of fixations determines the efficiency of a student's visual and perceptual capability. The term fixation, or eye-stop, refers to that interval in reading a line of print during which the eye is held relatively stationary for a short time, and, during which, word perception takes place. The eye moves in this fashion across each line of print in a series of saccades, pausing after each saccade for a fixation and then sweeps back in another larger saccadic movement to the beginning of the next line of print. This longer eye movement is commonly referred to as a return sweep.

The majority of people are relatively unaware of the vast number of fixations they make in proportion to the amount of words read. (See Table 2.1.) For instance, the average adult reading a 10-word line will tend to make from 8–10 fixations. A superior reader will make perhaps 5, while a child in elementary school will fixate from 13–22 times in 10 words. The "word by word" reader does not make one eye-stop per word but usually makes two or more per word. We are unaware of this amount of activity because of the rapidity with which eye movements take place, the subtlety of the activity involved, and our lack of direct, conscious control of this process. Thus, eye-movement recording is the only means of studying the movement of the eyes during silent reading.

An individual might employ a comparatively large number of fixations in relation to grade level norms for either of the following reasons:

Table 2.1

Taylor National Norms														Advanced				
Grade Level	1	2	3	4	5	6	7	8	9	10	11	12	Col.	1	2	3	4	5
Fixations/100 words	224	174	155	139	129	120	114	109	105	101	96	94	90	77	65	57	48	44

"Grade Level Norms for the Components of the Fundamental Reading Skill," by Stanford E. Taylor, Helen Frackenpohl and James L. Pettee. EDL Research and Information Bulletin No. 3, Educational Developmental Laboratories, Inc., 1960. Advanced represents typical reading performance characteristics for trained readers.

1. **Difficulty with visual acuity or binocular coordination:** An inability to see well enough, or to coordinate the eyes properly to achieve good print resolution, will tend to increase the amount of fixations as well as regressions.

2. **Conditioning of early reading experiences:** An excessive number of fixations and regressions can become part of an individual's habitual reading performance through the conditioning that occurs during the early stages of learning to read and will be discussed in Chapters 4 and 5. An excessive number of fixations can become habitual because of the following:
   - There is often a considerable number of new words encountered each week in grades 1 through 3. Without "flash or automaticity training," word recognition is quite slow, which promotes considerable word scrutiny and results in nonfluent reading.
   - There is often an emphasis on oral reading, which can influence the reader's and the listener's viewing habits adversely, encouraging an excess number of fixations and regressions. Since oral reading is typically much slower and less fluent than silent reading, visual wandering is encouraged.
   - There is occasionally an overstress on phonics, which can condition an interruption of the fluent reading process that results in an increased number of fixations and regressions if words are habitually and unnecessarily analyzed.
   - There are difficulties with comprehension as well as a lack of confidence in the ability to understand satisfactorily during reading. This can result in a wandering and rereading manner of reading.

All of these early learning experiences can contribute to a less than fluent approach to silent reading, which often becomes incorporated into a rather habitual oculomotor activity that is inefficient by the intermediate grades, as described in Chapter 4.

It is a well-established fact that a more efficient reader requires fewer fixations in reading a given line of print than a poorer reader. Certainly, it is desirable to acquire visual/functional and perceptual habits and cognitive competence that result in a minimum amount of ocular activity. Generally, the greater the number of fixations, the more time is spent in reading, the greater the task of understanding, and, ultimately, the greater the expenditure of energy that is required by the reading process.

Regressions

Regressions, or reverse fixations, are those fixations that occur following a right-to-left saccade or interfixation movement. Excessive regressions can result from less than satisfactory visual acuity or binocular coordination problems, conditioning during "beginning-to-read" stages, perceptual inadequacies, as well as poor or unsatisfactory comprehension.

Sometimes habitual regressions result from the inadequate formation of good directional attack. When learning to read, the person tends to incorporate or employ a certain amount of corrective movement in each line of print. Many times this habit is so ingrained that regressions will occur at similar points in every line of print.

Many individuals incorporate a number of regressions into their reading performance because of a lack of confidence and an ingrained need to "double-check" words. (See Table 2.2.) Their general insecurity in terms of remembering what they have read is sufficiently great to cause them to regress and, at times, even reread portions of lines or whole sections of a selection habitually.

Regressions require only fractions of a second (perhaps only .24 seconds) and, because they are interspersed with forward fixations, the reader is seldom conscious of their occurrence. Although the time required for a single regression is small, total time spent in regressions might occupy from one-fifth to one-third of the total reading time. Desirably, the proportion of regressions to total fixations should not exceed 10–15 percent.

A more efficient reader will make fewer regressions in reading than a poorer reader and will exhibit a more efficient directional attack, which results in more sequential input of information to short-term memory.

Average Span of Recognition

The span of recognition refers to the amount of words or word-parts perceived during a fixation or eye-pause during reading. Span of recognition

Table 2.2

Taylor National Norms														Advanced			
Grade Level	1	2	3	4	5	6	7	8	9	10	11	12	Col.	1	2	3	4	5
Percentage of Regressions/100 words	52	40	35	31	28	25	23	21	20	19	18	17	15	11	8	5	4	2

"Grade Level Norms for the Components of the Fundamental Reading Skill," by Stanford E. Taylor, Helen Frackenpohl and James L. Pettee. EDL Research and Information Bulletin No. 3, Educational Developmental Laboratories, Inc., 1960. Advanced represents typical reading performance characteristics for trained readers.

does not refer to the amount of material impinging on the retina of the eye but rather to the amount the reader recognizes or can deal with interpretively. In reading, the "perceptions" are so interrelated and interdependent that it is unrealistic to think of span of recognition as a measurement during an isolated seeing situation. Instead, when considering a person's visual intake in reading, one must look at the total number of fixations required to read 100 words to judge a reader's performance throughout a selection as providing a more typical reflection of his or her average visual intake or typical "salvageable" span. (See the following illustration.)

The average span of recognition is determined by noting the number of fixations required to read a designated number of words. In a Visagraph® recording, the average span of recognition data is indicated fully realizing that there is undoubtedly some variation in span of recognition from fixation to fixation.

Table 2.3 indicates that a first grader at the end of the academic year perceives an average of only .45 of a word per eye-stop. Students do not average a full word until eleventh grade and the average college student averages only 1.11 words while reading at the rate of 280 words per minute. Even after fluency development training, the span for a good reader seldom exceeds 2.5 words. A key limiting factor is the relatively small amount of print that can be seen with good legibility. As described in Chapter 1, studies by Feinberg (1949) and Legge, Cheung, Yu, Chung, Lee, and Owens, (2007) show how there is a substantial falloff of the clarity of vision from the reader's fixation point while reading.

It is apparent, then, that phrase-seeing during reading is a myth. Realizing, however, that all readers, even beginners in first grade, "think" in phrases and larger linguistic units, one can only conclude that a person con-

Table 2.3

Taylor National Norms																	
													Advanced				
Grade Level	1	2	3	4	5	6	7	8	9	10	11	12	Col.	1	2	3	4	5
Average Span of Recognition in Words	.45	.57	.65	.72	.78	.83	.88	.92	.95	.99	1.04	1.06	1.11	1.30	1.53	1.75	2.08	2.27

"Grade Level Norms for the Components of the Fundamental Reading Skill," by Stanford E. Taylor, Helen Frackenpohl and James L. Pettee. EDL Research and Information Bulletin No. 3. Educational Developmental Laboratories, Inc., 1960. Advanced represents typical reading performance characteristics for trained readers.

structs a thought or idea through a series of eye-stops or visual impressions as these impressions are processed in short-term memory.

Average Duration of Fixation

The duration of fixation refers to the length of time a reader's eyes pause during a fixation. In a Visagraph® eye-movement recording, the term "average duration of fixation" is computed from the time (in seconds) it takes a reader to read the selection and the total number of fixations employed in reading the selection.

The following norm chart (Table 2.4) indicates that an elementary school child might pause as long as .33 seconds per eye-stop, making about three movements per second. (This is undoubtedly influenced by the fact that the reading experience is predominantly oral, the child does not recognize a great many words easily and quickly, and the child does not associate very rapidly.) The college student, a more mature reader, might average only .24 seconds per eye-stop, or slightly more than four fixations per second.

In general, duration of fixation tends to shorten as an individual matures, reflecting a decrease in reaction time and an increase in the rapidity with which the reader recognizes words, associates, and comprehends. The chart, however, indicates the duration changes only slightly after the child reaches fourth grade or 10 to 11 years of age.

Reading Rate With Comprehension

The term "rate" refers to the time required by a reader to read through a given selection with adequate comprehension.

A measurement of rate of words per minute has the most significance when it refers to a usual manner of reading, or the way the person might typically read a magazine, novel, or other nontest material where rereading or reflection are at a minimal level. Rather than referring to a skimming rate where only portions of the context are read, or a reflective or analytical read-

Table 2.4

Taylor National Norms																	
														Advanced			
Grade Level	1	2	3	4	5	6	7	8	9	10	11	12	Col.	1	2	3	4	5
Average Duration of Fixation (seconds)	.33	.30	.28	.27	.27	.27	.27	.27	.27	.26	.26	.25	.24	.23	.23	.22	.22	.22

"Grade Level Norms for the Components of the Fundamental Reading Skill," by Stanford E. Taylor, Helen Frackenpohl and James L. Pettee. EDL Research and Information Bulletin No. 3, Educational Developmental Laboratories, Inc., 1960. Advanced represents typical reading performance characteristics for trained readers.

ing that requires rereading or pauses to reflect and perhaps visualize, it is more meaningful to refer to a person's "usual" rate, a rate at which narrative-informational material is read. This is the manner of rate referred to as "rate with comprehension" in Visagraph® recordings.

While rate cannot be considered apart from comprehension, there are certain factors that greatly influence the relative rapidity with which a reader deals with print. Among these will be a reader's visual/functional efficiency perceptual accuracy, and information processing efficiency; all facets of an oculomotor activity which have become habitual through the years. These factors prevent rate from being directly proportional to the difficulty of the content, to the experiences of the reader, or to the comprehension achieved. In other words, many people, particularly poorer or less efficient readers, will not vary greatly in their reading rate on different levels of material unless the difficulty of the material becomes overwhelming. Other readers' comprehension will be poor no matter how slowly they read. In addition, there are readers whose comprehension improves as they consciously attempt to increase their rate and others whose comprehension drops.

Many persons assume that rate is a highly variable factor and that they can, at will, alter their rate to suit the situation or purpose. In actuality, the vast majority of people vary their rate only slightly on material that could be classified as easy to fairly difficult.

Table 2.5 indicates the average rate demonstrated by students at various levels when reading material at their grade level. In addition, the average adult has been found to read at rates ranging from 175 to 300 words per minute, with a more typical or average rate of 225 words per minute. The superior adult reader might average 500 words per minute and even the best readers, after completing a reading improvement course, rarely read above rates of 650 words per minute.

Table 2.5

Taylor National Norms													Advanced				
Grade Level	1	2	3	4	5	6	7	8	9	10	11	12	Col.	1	2	3	4	5
WPM Rate w/Comprehension	80	115	138	158	173	185	195	204	214	224	237	250	280	340	400	480	560	620

"Grade Level Norms for the Components o the fundamental Reading Skill," by Stanford e. Taylor, Helen Frackenpohl and James L. Pettee. EDL Research and Information Bulletin No. 3, Educational Developmental Laboratories, Inc., 1960. Advanced represents typical reading performance characteristics for trained readers.

Reading Rate Without Rereading

This rate provides helpful information in comparing a subject's performance in pre/post tests where one Visagraph® test involved rereading. This allows a more equivalent comparison of reading performance efficiency. The rate with comprehension will include any rereading performances. The rate adjusted for rereading, however, is a calculation that eliminates any effect of rereading. Any intraline rereading (instances in which a regressive movement is greater than 30 percent of the line value, which typically exceeds usual regressive activity) and any extra lines read by a student are deleted in this calculation.

Directional Attack Difficulty

The term "directional attack" refers to the characteristic tendency of the reader to perceive and organize content in a left-to-right manner. The perceptual activity and ocular patterns in reading are so interrelated that it may be said that the recorded pattern indicates, in a general manner, both the perceptual accuracy of the individual and his or her orderliness in dealing with the content. Thus, the pattern made by the reader's eyes reveals the quality and nature of his or her directional attack and is as individualistic as are the components themselves.

The quality of a reader's directional attack relates directly to the manner in which information is fed into short-term memory. When visual impressions are sequential and regular it can be assumed that the impressions being processed in short-term memory are likewise sequential and reinforcing syntactically as a result. By contrast, poor directional attack would suggest a more imperfect nonsyntactical and less reinforcing word input into short-term memory.

Directional Attack Difficulty, as a calculation of the percentage of regressions to total fixations, is automatically provided by the Visagraph®. Generally, should the percentage of regressions to fixations be 10–15 percent or less, a reader's directional attack can be judged relatively efficient. If the percentage is 25 percent or more, the reader is employing a poor directional attack.

Grade Level Efficiency

The Visagraph® will automatically calculate a reader's relative reading efficiency and resulting equivalent grade level efficiency (GLE) performance.

The grade level efficiency of a subject's reading performance is a calculation made on the basis of a student's rate and the amount of visual activity to achieve this rate. GLE is based on the following considerations:

- It presupposes that fixations, regressions and rate are the most important components (span and duration being calculations derived from these).
- It presupposes that a person who makes more fixations and regressions is generally less effective perceptually. Regressions are given additional weight in the calculations (they are already included in the total count of fixations).

Cross-Correlation

Although the cross-correlation report is designed to evaluate adequacy of binocular coordination, a very low cross-correlation (perhaps .75 or lower) may signify the need for another recording. A low cross-correlation can be caused by a poor recording when the IPDs of the Visagraph® goggles, which determine the position of the infrared emitters and sensors, are set improperly. A confirmation of the adequacy of a recording can be made by comparing the Original Graph with the Model Graph. If they seem very similar, the recording is probably satisfactory and the cross-correlation is probably low because of coordination difficulties. Generally, a cross-correlation of less than 90 percent is cause for concern.

Grade Norms–Normative Performance

The profile plot, shown in the report on page 50, displays a subject's reading performance characteristics in relation to Taylor norms. The lines to the right indicate the extent to which performance exceeds grade norms and the lines to the left indicate performance less than grade level expectations.

Grade Norm/Goal

The reading performance characteristics are displayed against Grade Norms and Goals. The Goals represent the minimum performances that would be expected from a reading fluency development training program if an individual were reading with grade level normative behavior.

Comprehension Questions Correct

As mentioned previously, the comprehension score is primarily used to qualify that the subject was reading in a usual or typical manner. A score of 70 percent or higher comprehension is acceptable. If the comprehension score is 60 percent or lower, another recording should be administered either using a lower-level test selection (perhaps 1–2 levels lower) or cautioning a student to read more carefully.

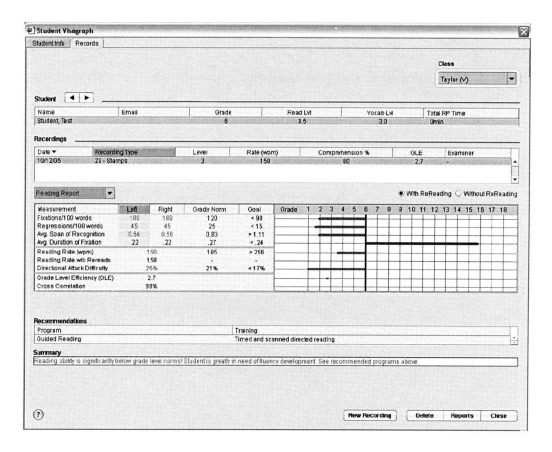

Interpreting the Reading Simulation

The Simulation is a graphic depiction of the manner in which a student traverses each line of text. Viewing the simulation is extremely informative and motivational for students, teachers, and parents as they view the considerable amount of visual activity during the reading process.

A colored band moves across the text, as shown in the following report, to simulate the subject's eye-movement performance on the test selection at his or her reading rate.

This display does not plot exact fixation locations but does reasonably depict all fixations and regressions made on all lines displayed as well as the duration of each fixation.

Many students are startled by the amount of visual activity they employed in silent reading. At this time, the examiner can point out that their reading performance is simply how they learned to read and that this process can be improved easily through fluency in silent reading training. So many

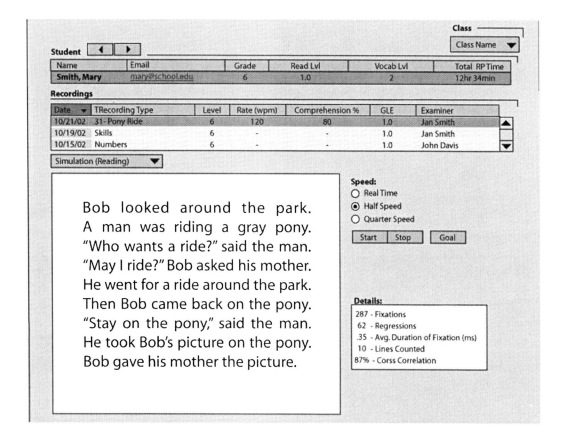

students then realize that they are not "dumb" but are simply in need of training to read in a more efficient manner. This is quite a relief to them. As an example, one 15-year-old student in New York City who had completed a Visagraph® recording asked, "Can I have a copy of this to show my mother?" When asked why, the student replied, "I never realized how I was reading."

Interpreting the Visual Functional Report

Many students will experience difficulty in reading because of poorly developed visual/functional competencies (binocular coordination and vergence, ocular motility and tracking). The Visagraph® is invaluable in that it allows an examiner to screen for possible visual impediments. (See the following report.) If a student exhibits many symptoms (indicated in red), he or she should be referred to a qualified vision specialist for a more complete visual diagnosis. The factors that should be reviewed are as follows:

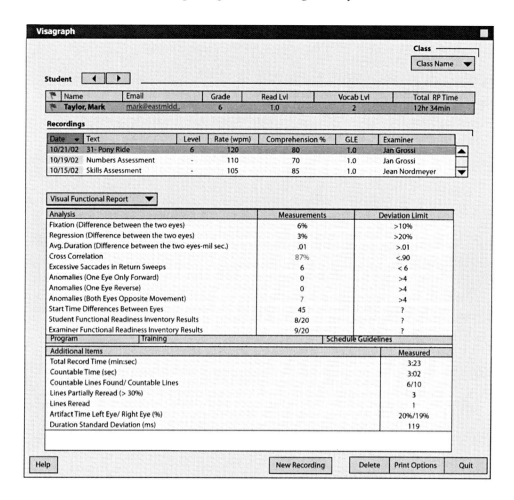

Fixations (Difference Between the Two Eyes)

In most instances, the performance of a subject's two eyes will be quite similar. However, in instances where the difference in total fixations for both eyes exceeds 10 percent, there may be an indication of binocular coordination difficulty.

Regressions (Difference Between the Two Eyes)

As with fixations, any difference that exceeds 20 percent may also indicate difficulty with binocular coordination.

Average Duration (Difference Between the Two Eyes–mil. sec.)

A difference of .01 between the two eyes may also be another indicator of binocular coordination difficulty.

Cross-Correlation

Cross-correlation indicates the degree to which the interfixational saccades of the two eyes are similar in excursion throughout the reading. A perfect correlation would be 1.000. Less than this would indicate some degree of difference in the similarity of saccades of the two eyes in either interfixation movement and/or return sweeps. Low correlations can be significant and need to be studied. It is likely that a correlation less than .90 is suspect.

Excessive Saccades in Return Sweeps

Ideally, the number of return sweep saccades will equal the number of lines found. Any excess return sweep saccades indicate compensating movements made during the process of executing a return sweep. If a student's coordination or tracking is poor, the number of saccades in return sweeps can, at times, be two or perhaps three or more times the number of lines found. Excessive return sweeps greater than the lines found is another red flag," that might indicate inadequate visual functioning.

Anomalies

If more than four anomalies are reported (in red), this could also signal visual/function difficulties. These numbers reflect the following:

- The first anomaly number indicates instances in which one eye moved in a forward direction and the other eye (either eye) did not move substantially enough to be recognized as a forward fixation. (The amount of movement to identify a movement as a new fixation is 2 percent of the total average line value. This is roughly equivalent to one to two letter spaces.)
- The second anomaly number indicates instances in which one eye moved in a reverse direction and the other eye did not move sufficiently to be detected as a new regressive fixation.
- The third anomaly number indicates the instances in which the two eyes appear to move in opposite directions. Whenever this occurs, it is best to examine the subject's Original Graph to be sure that the reported differences in the two eyes are truly significant.

Start-Time Differences Between Eyes

The nature of start-time differences between the two eyes is counted and reported. To date, however, there is no criteria as to the number of start-time differences that might support the consideration that differences in start time reflect a coordination difficulty. An excessive number of such instances in conjunction with other reported data will simply add to an indication of visual/functional difficulty.

ADMINISTERING THE STUDENT/EXAMINER FUNCTIONAL READINESS INVENTORY

As mentioned previously in Chapter 1, when there are reasons to suspect that a student's visual function is not adequate (low cross-correlation, excessive return sweeps, anomalies, etc.), a Functional Readiness Inventory should be administered. The Student Inventory Questions, shown in the following image, reflect a student's awareness of any visual/functional problems, which will often support the numerical findings revealed by the Visagraph®.

In instances where parent or teacher responses can be obtained, the Teacher Inventory Questions shown on page 56 are administered to further support an evaluation of a student's visual/functional difficulties.

Obviously, the greater the number of adverse responses by a student or examiner, the greater the possibility that the student is experiencing visual/functional difficulty and the greater likelihood of the need for referral to a vision specialist.

EXAMINING THE READING GRAPHS

Two types of reading graphs are available: a Model Graph and an Original Graph. The Original Graph is an exact plot of a position of the two eyes every .167 milliseconds throughout the student's reading. The Model Graph is a recast of this data to depict the movement of the eyes in terms of a reasonably significant shift of fixation, 2.8 percent of the average return sweep, or 2–3 letters of excursion. The graph shown on page 57 indicates the nature of the data that supplements the graphic depiction.

Reading Plus®
Visagraph® Student Inventory Questions

1. Do you like to read?
2. Do you get headaches when reading?
3. Can you read easily for 15 minutes?
4. Can you read easily for 30 minutes?
5. Can you read easily for 1 hour?
6. Can you read easily for 2 hours?
7. Do you get tired and sleepy when you read?
8. Do you study in short spurts?
9. Do your eyes get tired while reading?
10. Do your eyes get itchy while reading?
11. Do your eyes ever burn while reading?
12. Do your eyes get watery during reading?
13. Do the words in reading ever get muddy or blurred?
14. Do the letters in words double up or wiggle at times?
15. Do you find yourself saying the words to yourself during reading?
16. Do you have trouble understanding what you read?
17. Do you ever get car sick or headaches riding in a car?
18. Do you get a stiff neck or backache after reading?
19. Do you find your eyes bother you in sports such as baseball, basketball, tennis, or ping pong?
20. Do you feel your reading can be improved?

Reading Plus®

Visagraph® Teacher Inventory Questions

1. Is student's level of academic achievement satisfactory for his/her age and/or grade?

2. Has progress been satisfactory in reading?

3. Has the student repeated any grade?

4. Is the student interested in school?

5. Does the student fatigue easily during reading and study tasks?

6. Is there a tendency to study in spurts?

7. Is there a tendency for the student to be easily distracted during reading?

8. Does the student seem to be happy and well adjusted in the school environment?

9. Does the student attend school regularly?

10. Does he/she squint, blink, close or cover one eye at either close or distant viewing tasks?

11. During reading, is there a tendency to skip words, insert incorrect words or guess at words?

12. Does the student use a finger frequently to keep his/her place during reading?

13. Does the student frequently lose his/her place during reading?

14. Is there a tendency to tilt the head during reading?

15. Does the student draw in closer than 10 inches when reading?

16. Is there a tendency for one eye to turn in or out during reading?

17. Is there a considerable head movement during reading?

18. Is there a tendency to vocalize during reading?

19. Does the student develop red eyes or encrusted lids (exclusive of instances of infection)?

20. Does the student complain frequently about reading and study tasks being too time consuming?

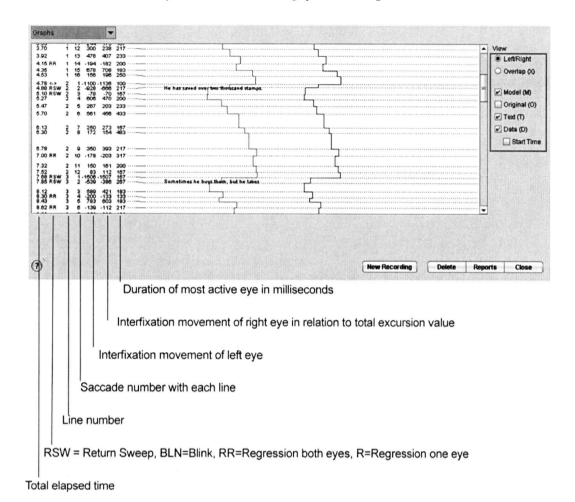

Duration of most active eye in milliseconds

Interfixation movement of right eye in relation to total excursion value

Interfixation movement of left eye

Saccade number with each line

Line number

RSW = Return Sweep, BLN=Blink, RR=Regression both eyes, R=Regression one eye

Total elapsed time

All of the visual performance characteristics displayed in the Model and Original Graphs are depicted in the following example.

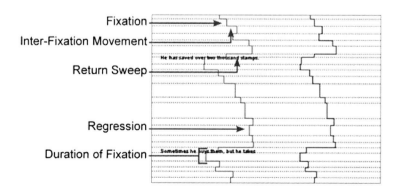

If you were to examine the Original graphs, which provide the basis for the conversion to the Model graph (realigned for a clearer portrayal of the fixations and regressions), one can learn even more about the visual/functional competence of a subject.

Vergence–In the Original Graph, as shown in the following image, one can examine vergence or the student's ability to coordinate and use both eyes as a team. If, for example, one eye holds steady and vertical during a fixation and the other seems to sway sideways, there could be a problem in a student's holding vergence and fusing the images of both eyes. The angling out of both eyes during a fixation also indicates a tendency for the student to lose vergence after fixating his or her eyes.

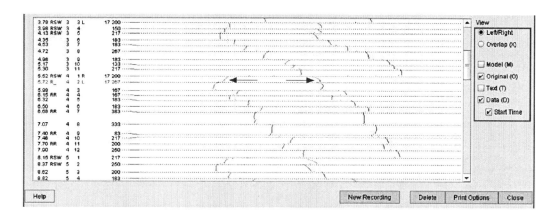

Head Sway–When both eyes are swaying in the same direction, as depicted in the following graph, the student is moving his or her head during reading. This is not a loss of binocular control.

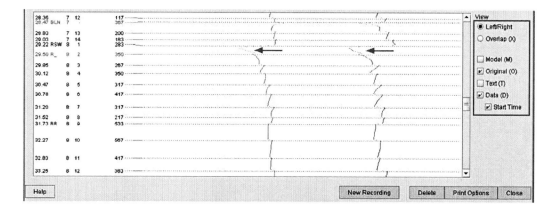

Anomalies–Anomalies are instances in which one eye (either eye) moves in a forward or reverse manner, as shown in the following graph, and the other eye does not move, or when both eyes move in different directions to a new fixation point.

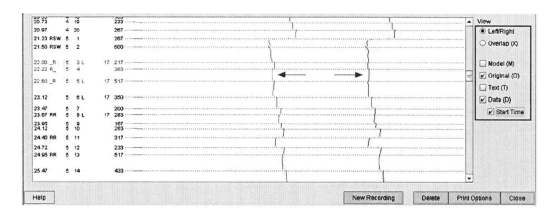

Blink–A blink (designated as BLN) is detected when both eyes move radically in opposite directions and then swing back as in the following graph. A blink is nonanalyzed time and in the final calculations this time interval is extrapolated to the usual number of fixations and regressions that would have occurred during this interval of time. A few blinks are not unusual, however, excessive blinking could be an additional sign of visual discomfort.

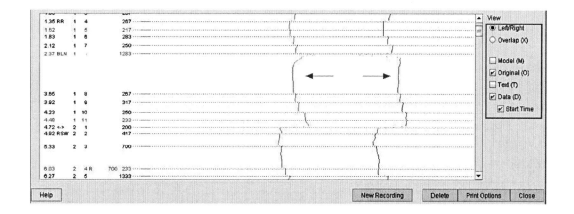

CONCLUSION

As you can see, the amount of data concerning "how" a student reads in terms of fluency or efficiency can be secured objectively and quite easily through an eye-movement recording system. The number of fixations and regressions a reader executes, average duration of fixation, and his or her reading rate determines the degree of reading efficiency or fluency during silent reading. Since the eye moves from three to five times per second, the only reliable means of evaluating a reader's oculomotor efficiency is through eye-movement recording. This data can also suggest the degree of need for fluency development training, and following training a post eye-movement recording can indicate the degree of improvement in a student's silent reading efficiency. Adding this information to a student's achievement test data, which determines reading effectiveness, can provide a more complete evaluation of both his or her efficiency and effectiveness in silent reading.

Further, should there be a difference in the performance of the two eyes and adverse responses to the Student and Teacher Questionnaires, it is possible that the student should be referred to a vision specialist to check both vision and visual functioning.

QUESTIONS THAT MAY ARISE
AFTER READING THIS CHAPTER

1. With whom should eye-movement recordings be used and how best to accomplish this?
2. How can eye-movement recordings be scheduled, perhaps initially with vision screening in a school?
3. Who should administer a Visagraph® recording, and who will interpret the information and relate the results to reading remediation or development?
4. How often should eye-movement recordings be made of a student to document change and progress in oculomotor development (a reflection of visual/functional, perceptual and information processing proficiency)?

There has been extensive reading research involving eye-movement recording over the years. The following listings under References can further an understanding and appreciation of this aspect of reading and its role in helping students to achieve silent reading fluency.

REFERENCES

Though only three of these references are referred to in Chapter 2, the additional studies and publications are important as historical references with regard to eye-movement recording and the reading process.

Ballantine, F. A. (1951). Age changes in measures of eye movements in silent reading. In *Studies of the psychology of reading.* (Monographs in Education, No. 4, pp. 67–111). Ann Arbor: University of Michigan Press.

Buswell, G. T. (1922). Fundamental reading habits: A study of their development. *Supplementary Educational Monographs, No. 21* (pp. xiv + 150). Chicago: University of Chicago Press.

Carmichael, L., & Dearborn, W. F. (1947). *Reading and visual fatigue.* Boston: Houghton Mifflin Company.

Dearborn, W. F. (1906). The psychology of reading, Columbia University *Contributions to Philosophy, Psychology and Education, 14*(1). Also listed in Archives of Philosophy. *Psychology and Scientific Methods, 4* (p. 134). New York: Columbia University Press.

Delabarre, E. B. (1898). A method of recording eye-movements. *American Journal of Psychology, 9,* 572–574.

Dodge, R. (1907). An experimental study of visual fixation. *Psychological Monograph, 8,* 1–95.

Dodge, R., & Clive, T. C. (1901, March). The angle velocity of eye-movements. *Psychological Review, 8,* 145–157.

Feinberg, R. (1949, March). A study of some aspects of peripheral visual acuity. *American Journal of Optometry and Archives of American Academy of Optometrics, 26,* 49–56.

George, E. J., Toren J. A., & Lowell, J. W. (1923). Study of the ocular movements in the horizontal plane. *American Journal of Ophthalmology, 6,* 833–838.

Gilbert, D. W. (1956). *Power and speed in reading* (pp. 106–110). Englewood Cliffs, NJ: Prentice-Hall.

Gilbert, L. C. (1940, April). Effect on silent reading of attempting to follow oral reading. *Elementary School Journal, 40,* 614–621.

Gilbert, L. C. (1959, February). Saccadic movements as a factor in visual perception in reading. *Journal of Educational Psychology, 50,* 15–19.

Gilbert, L. C. (1959, February). Speed of processing visual stimuli and its relation to reading. *Journal of Educational Psychology, 50,* 8–14.

Gilbert, L. C., & Gilbert, D. W. (1942). Reading before the eye-movement camera versus reading away from it. *Elementary School Journal, 42,* 443–447.

Guilford, J. B., & Hackman, R. B. (1936). Varieties and levels of clearness correlated with eye movements. *American Journal of Psychology, 48,* 371–388.

Hoffman, A. C., Wellman, B., & Carmichael, L. (1939). A quantitative comparison of the electrical and photographic techniques of eye-movement recording. *Journal of Experimental Psychology, 24,* 40–53.

Javal, L. E. (1879). Essai sur la Physiologie de la lecture. *Annales d'Oculistique, 82,* 242–253.

Just, M. A., & Carpenter, P. A. (1980). A theory of reading: From eye fixations to comprehension. *Psychological Review, 87,* 329–354.

Legge, G. E., Cheung, S.-H., Yu, D., Chung, S. T. L., Lee, H.-W., & Owens, D. P. (2007). The case for the visual span as a sensory bottleneck in reading. *Journal of Vision, 7*(2):9, 1–15.

McConkie, G. W. (1983). *Eye-movements and perception during reading: Eye movements in reading, perceptual and language processes* (pp. 65–96). New York: Academic Press, Inc.

McConkie, G. W., & Rayner, K. (1975). The span of the effective stimulus during a fixation in reading. *Perception & Psychophysics, 17*(6), 578–586.

McConkie, G. W., & Rayner, K. (1976). Asymmetry of the perceptual span of reading. *Bulletin of the Psychonomic Society, 8,* 365–368.

Morris, H. F. (1973). *Eye-movement analysis with the Reading Eye II.* New York: EDL/McGraw-Hill.

Morse, W. C. (1951). Comparisons of the eye movements of fifth and seventh grade pupils reading materials of corresponding difficulty. In *Studies in the Psychology of Reading. Monographs in Education, No. 4* (pp. 3–64). Ann Arbor: University of Michigan Press.

Paterson, D. G., & Tinker, M. A. (1940). Influence of line width on eye-movements. *Journal of Experimental Psychology, 27,* 572–577.

Paulson, E. J., & Feeman, A. E. (2003). *Insight from the eyes: The science of effective reading instruction.* Portsmouth, NH: Heinemann.

Rayner, K. (1983). *Eye movements in reading, perceptual language processes.* New York: Academic Press, Inc.

Rayner, K. (1993). Eye movements in reading: Recent developments. *Current Directions in Psychological Science, 2,* 81–86.

Starr, M. S., & Rayner, K. (2001, April). Eye movements during reading: Some current controversies. *Trends in Cognitive Sciences, 5*(4), 156–163.

Taylor, E. A. (1937). *Controlled reading.* Chicago: University of Chicago Press.

Taylor, E. A. (1957, October). The spans: Perception, apprehension and recognition. *American Journal of Ophthalmology, 44,* 501–507.

Taylor, E. A. (1966). *The fundamental reading skill* (2nd ed., pp. xviii–157). Springfield, IL: Charles C Thomas.

Taylor, S. E. (1960). *Eye-movement photography with the Reading Eye.* Huntington, NY: Educational Development Laboratories, Inc.

Taylor, S. E. (1971). *The dynamic activity of reading.* Huntington, NY: EDL/McGraw-Hill.

Taylor, S. E., & Frackenpohl, H. (1952). *Controlled exposure.* Huntington, NY: Educational Developmental Laboratories, Inc.

Taylor, S. E., Frackenpohl, H., & Pettee, J. L. (1960). Grade level norms for the components of the fundamental reading skill. *EDL Research and Information Bulletin, 3.* New York: EDL/McGraw Hill.

Tinker, M. A. (1929). Photographic measures of reading ability. *Journal of Educational Psychology 20*(3), 184–191.

Chapter 3

TECHNOLOGY'S ROLE IN SILENT READING FLUENCY DEVELOPMENT

Stanford E. Taylor

Since the introduction of the first reading training device in the 1930s, three major forms of technology have been employed to improve the more basic visual and perceptual processes of reading. These techniques are designed to improve automaticity of word recognition as well as the nature of the input process of words into short-term memory, which initiates understanding.

It is estimated that between 1960 and the year 2000, over 50 million students were trained with many of these earlier techniques. Today, millions more are enjoying the benefits of online computer techniques to improve their silent reading efficiency and attain greater proficiency in reading. Results of these training techniques are briefly described in Chapters 4 and 5.

In the past, two major forms of technology were used to develop silent reading fluency: tachistoscopic (flash) devices and controlled reading or guided reading instrumentation.

Tachistoscopic devices present numbers, letters, or words for brief intervals (perhaps 1/10 of a second or faster) to develop orthographic (letter configuration) competence and word recognition automaticity. When readers can rapidly recognize words in this short interval of time during their usual duration of fixation, they leave some time during each fixation to devote to word association (phrasing) and comprehension.

Controlled reading or guided reading devices present continuous text in a left-to-right timed manner to provide visual and perceptual modeling practice that allows students to improve their *Fundamental Reading Process,* which encompasses:

- visual/functional competence (binocular coordination, ocular motility, and accuracy in tracking)
- perceptual accuracy (letter and letter order recognition, word recognition automaticity, and visual memory)
- information processing efficiency (rate and improved sequence of word input into short-term memory).

This chapter will not cover what are termed "reading rate accelerators," such as the *Rateometer* and *Shadowscope,* since these are simply timing devices that do not provide any form of training that will modify basic visual and perceptual behavior. Gelzer and Santore (1968) conducted a study that concluded that timing techniques did not provide lasting improvements in reading rate, oculomotor behavior, and achievement as measured by both eye-movement recording and standardized tests.

TACHISTOSCOPIC DEVICES

The Merriam-Webster Medical Dictionary defines a tachistoscope as "an apparatus for the brief exposure of visual stimuli that is used in the study of learning, attention, and perception." A more specific definition of a tachistoscope should cite the capability of presenting images for one-sixth of a second or less, an interval of time that does not allow more than a single fixation in which to perceive. Thus, the goal of tachistoscopic training is to reduce the time interval spent on word recognition in each fixation so that some time in each fixation can be devoted to word association and comprehension.

The first tachistoscopic (timed exposure) technique was described by A.W. Volkmann (1859); however, flash training did not receive much recognition until World War II, when this type of training was used to instruct fighter pilots to rapidly identify aircraft silhouettes as friend or foe.

One of the first commercially available tachistoscopes used for training rapid word and phrase recognition was the *Flashmeter* in the 1940s. The Flashmeter, manufactured by Keystone View of Meadview, Pennsylvania, was an overhead projector that used glass slides and made timed exposures through the use of a camera shutter.

The Flashmeter purported to develop "phrase seeing" in reading, a training goal that was later disproven. Robinson (1934) and later Taylor (1957) both clarified in their reports that span of recognition was different for tachistoscopic exposures than in continuous reading. If someone could perceive two to four word phrases during continuous reading, the person's reading rate would be one thousand words per minute or higher, according to Taylor (1957). Very few highly skilled readers can read at this rate, and the average student is almost certainly unable to achieve this rate in reading.

Multiple reasons explain the greater span of recognition that is possible during tachistoscopic exposures. First, there is the unusually high level of attention generated just prior to a flashed exposure, which is far greater than the level of attention that can be maintained during continuous reading. Second, with camera shutter exposures there is typically the ability to use an after-image following the exposure. Third, there is no overlap of successive impressions as occurs in usual reading. Regardless, tachistoscopic training can focus on developing orthographic competence, word recognition automaticity, and visual memory, all necessary competencies that permit silent reading fluency to emerge. As mentioned earlier, developing these competencies allows a reader to perceive words rapidly and accurately during only a portion of his or her usual duration of fixation, which allows time for comprehension.

In the 1950s, the Chicago-based Society of Visual Education (SVE) released the *Spedioscope,* a device that used a filmstrip projector equipped with a camera shutter to present timed exposures. (See the following image.) This training program also purported to develop phrase seeing, but it did accomplish the goal of developing word recognition automaticity.

In the late 1950s, the *Tach-X* (originally named the *Timex*), was developed by this author and was released by Educational Developmental Laboratories (EDL) of Huntington, New York. This group-training device employed a motor to drive the projector lens in and out of focus. (See the following image.) This provided a unique method of producing timed exposures by presenting letters, numbers, and words through an in-and-out of focus exposure technique. The initial image was out of focus, then brought into focus for a timed interval, and then returned to an out-of-focus state. With this form of exposure, there is constant light before, during, and following an exposure, eliminating any possible use of an after-image. Further, the blurring out of an image after the exposure was more similar to what occurs in continuous reading. With the Tach-X, phrase training was dismissed, and the focus was now on letter and number orthographic competence and word recognition competency. Tach-X training focused on developing instant word recognition with a controlled, high frequency vocabulary, especially in grades 1 through 3.

The chief limitation of group tachistoscopic training was the need to provide exposures for students with varying perceptual capabilities. A solution proposed by the Tach-X program, provided exposures containing one more set of numbers or letters in a group that would challenge the best perceiver. (See the following image.) All other students were told to focus on seeing just one more element than they had previously been able to achieve. Students then wrote what they could remember. Word recognition did not pose the same perceptual limitation, but students who could not see, retain, and write the word completely were told to write as much as they could remember of the word being exposed from left to right.

Shortly after the release of the *Tach-X,* EDL released its *Flash-X,* hand-held, individual tachistoscope. (See the following image.) This device utilized round cards containing numbers, letters, and words. These cards were inserted into the device and their content was exposed at one-sixth of a second or faster. This device also maintained a constant level of illumination before, during, and after an exposure.

In the 1970s, a *Tach-Mate* group training tachistoscope was released by Instructional/Communications Technology (ICT) of Huntington, New York. (See the following image.) The Tach-Mate also employed in-and-out of focus exposures of numbers, letters, and words. However, this device did not use a motor to drive the lens in and out of focus, but instead used a simple lever that dropped from an elevated and out-of-focus position through a focused position to a lower, out-of-focus position, providing one-sixth of a second exposures in clear focus. Students again wrote out what they could retain from what was flashed.

Later, ICT released the *Vu Mate* handheld individual tachistoscope. The Vu Mate flashed numbers, letters, and ICT's core vocabulary on cards at timed speeds of one-tenth of a second to one-hundredth of a second. (See the following image.)

The Vu Mate was eventually replaced by a simple lever tachistoscopic device that made exposures by flipping a lever. (See the following image.) This device was placed on training material booklets and moved downward from exposure to exposure in the booklet.

Today, tachistoscopic training is accomplished by computer software such as provided in the *Reading Plus*® fluency development system (2010). Reading Plus® presents students with individualized flash-and-type keyword activities before the students read a text selection. Flash training helps build readiness for more rapid word recognition of the keywords that will be encountered when reading the selection. Younger students (in grades 1 to 3) using Reading Plus® are also presented with timed scan and flash activities with the Reading Plus® core vocabulary words to build automaticity with the vocabulary they will encounter frequently in everyday reading. Also, in the Reading Plus® system's vocabulary enhancement activities, flashing and typing new words help build orthographic competence with a newly acquired reading vocabulary.

CONTROLLED READING AND GUIDED READING

Controlled reading and guided reading techniques, in which text is displayed and removed in a left-to-right fashion as seen in the following image, are sometimes referred to as continuous tachistoscopic presentations. While this is true to a degree, the modeling visual and perceptual training provided during continuous reading allows these devices to develop much more than just rapid recognition of words.

the   largest   car-racing

Timed left-to-right presentation of text encourages students to modify the manner in which they read through modeling practice. This form of reading content presentation discourages or eliminates regressions (reverse eye movements), excessive fixations, and visual wandering. This presentation also shortens the duration of fixation (eye-pause time for perception), resulting in more rapid comprehensive reading. During this form of silent reading training, three subliminal areas of a student's Fundamental Reading Process are altered.

- Visual/functional skills (binocular coordination, ocular motility, and accuracy of tracking) improve.
- Perceptual skills (awareness of letter order, word recognition automaticity, and improved visual memory) become more rapid and accurate.

- Information processing (rate and sequence of word input into short-term memory) becomes more efficient.

Changes in these basic skills result in an overall change in a student's oculomotor activity during reading and overall reading proficiency. These changes will also facilitate increased reading rates, improved comprehension, and greater ease and comfort during reading.

The intake of words during the silent reading process is extremely rapid and subliminal (three to five eye movements and fixations per second). Thus, a teacher cannot direct this process and a student cannot control his or her reading behavior. For more than 75 years, reading technology has been the only direct and effective means of developing efficiency in this process. Technology to improve reading emerged in the 1930s, starting with mechanical devices, later changing to projection techniques, and today using computer software.

Computerized eye-movement recording techniques, such as those employed by the Visagraph®, have also evolved to allow teachers to easily and rapidly evaluate the efficiency of a student's Fundamental Reading Process.

Metronoscope and Opthalmograph

The first reading training device, the *Metronoscope* (shown in the following image), was developed in the 1930s by Earl A., James Y., and Carl C. Taylor of Educational Laboratories of Brownwood, Texas. The Metronoscope employed three windows, opening sequentially from left to right in a timed manner to encourage more sequential left-to-right perception of content and more rapid reading. Reading content was divided into phrases that appeared in each window. The display rate was increased gradually during training, and a teacher posed comprehension questions after each reading selection.

The *Opthalmograph,* the first portable eye-movement recording device to record a student's oculomotor activity on 35-millimeter film, was released by Educational Laboratories in the 1930s. (See the following image.) The Opthalmograph was used to document reading efficiency changes produced by the Metronoscope.

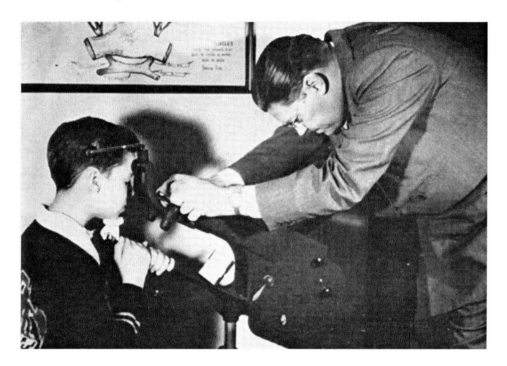

Harvard and Iowa Reading Films

During the late 1940s and into the 1950s, Harvard University and the University of Iowa released 16-millimeter motion picture training techniques that involved timed reading of selections to increase silent reading rate. These films employed left-to-right overlapping phrases. Limitations of these techniques included their phrase presentation, the lack of a library of graded reading selections, and the small number of training sessions primarily designed for the college level.

Controlled Reader and Reading Eye Camera

In the mid-1950s, S. E. Taylor of Educational Development Laboratories of Huntington, New York, introduced the *Controlled Reader* and the *Controlled Reader, Jr.* (See the following image.)

In 1960, S. E. Taylor introduced the Reading Eye eye-movement recording camera as shown in the following image.

Controlled reading provided left-to-right scanning of reading content in a timed manner to improve students' visual/functional, perceptual, and information processing skills that are needed for improved fluency in silent reading. The Controlled Reader unveiled and removed content in a continuous, guided manner, not phrased as with the Metronoscope or the Harvard and Iowa reading films. This guided manner of presenting print encouraged a student to move more sequentially and steadily in reading from left to right, eliminating nearly all regressions (right-to-left fixations) and the usual recovery process that follows regressions.

The *Prism Reader* also was introduced in the 1960s. (See the following image.) This device employed the Guided Reader equipped with *Risley Rotary Prisms* to develop binocular coordination and more rapid accommodation during the dynamic activity of reading, where students experience the greatest difficulty with visual coordination. This training was a distinct improvement over stationary stereoptic training in the development of fusion. Although it was hoped that such visual training would be instituted in schools, politics among vision specialists did not permit this to occur.

During the mid-1970s, the *Reading Eye* camera was replaced by the *Reading Eye II,* initially known as the *Eye Trac.* (See the following image.) The Reading Eye II recorded eye movements through the use of infrared sensors. Eye-movement recordings were made on heat-sensitive paper.

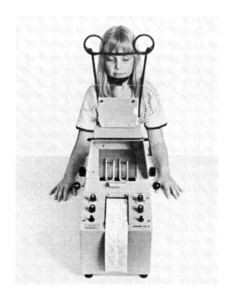

Guided Reader and Visagraph I

In the 1970s, Instructional Communications/Technology of Huntington, New York, released the *Guided Reader,* a projector that extended the legacy of the Controlled Reader. (See the following image.) As with the Controlled Reader, the Guided Reader projected continuous scanned, timed, left-to-right presentations of reading content. A unique improvement in the scanning illusion of the Guided Reader was the closing off of each line of print as well as the opening of the new line of print more rapidly, which tended to maintain a more continuous and fluent manner of reading. Comprehension questions were completed in study guides after each lesson.

The *Visagraph I,* the first computerized eye-movement recording device, was released in 1985. (See the following image.) The Visagraph recorded a student's silent reading using infrared sensors and emitters and automatically analyzed and calculated the number of fixations, regressions, duration of fixation, and reading rate exhibited by a student as he or she read.

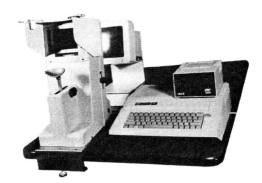

COMPUTERIZED GUIDED READING AND VISAGRAPH®

In the late 1990s, Guided Reading™ was introduced by Taylor Associates of Huntington, New York, as a component of the Reading Plus® software system. This manner of Guided Reading once again presented reading training content in a continuous left-to-right timed format similar to the techniques employed by the earlier Controlled Reader and Guided Reader. However, comprehension questions were presented on the screen and correction and reinforcement were presented as part of a Guided Reading™ lesson. Additionally, rereading and prereading provisions were provided. Perceptual accuracy and word recognition training were now part of this computerized routine.

In 1995, Taylor Associates released a new goggle version of an eye-movement recording device, the *Ober II: Visagraph.* (See the following image.)

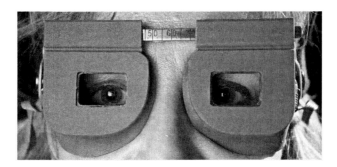

Later that same year, a *Visagraph® II* eye-movement recording technique was released, followed by the *Visagraph® III.* The Visagraph® system used a simplified pair of goggles that employed infrared sensors to record eye-movement behavior, documenting changes in silent reading fluency. (See the following image.) The use of goggles eliminated many of the problems of head movement during eye-movement recordings.

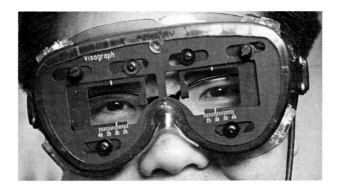

In 2007, Taylor Associates introduced an online web-based version of Guided Reading™. The following is an example of a typical reading lab. This version incorporated many automated features to create an individualized program for each student, and included provisions for scaffolding and scheduling of instruction. Now, Guided Reading™ automatically adjusts content level, lesson formats (length and type of presentation), rereading and prereading, as well as many motivating incentives, all based on a student's comprehension and reading rate. It also offers many essential reports for use by students, teachers, and administrators.

SUMMARY

Over the last 80 years a myriad of research, including studies that involve eye-movement recording, has proven conclusively the benefits of using reading technology to develop high levels of fluency in silent reading. A recent study by Rasinski, Samuels, Hiebert, Petscher, and Feller (2011) entitled "The Relationship Between a Silent Reading Fluency Instructional Protocol on Students' Reading Comprehension and Achievement in an Urban School Setting," included more than 16,000 students. It demonstrated conclusively that changes in the Fundamental Reading Process, as provided for in Guided

Reading™ in a scaffolding manner of practice, translate into improved scores on state reading achievement tests.

During this interval of time not one eye-movement study has been conducted that shows non-technological approaches to the development of silent reading fluency that are as successful as technological approaches in improving the subliminal high-speed process of silent reading.

In 2000, the National Reading Panel issued a report that addressed the need for developing fluency in oral reading, but did not include any studies that showed that oral reading development produced improvement in silent reading fluency or studies that were related to the development of silent reading fluency.

Silent reading proficiency is a critical skill used every day. It is an essential component of independent learning, a necessity for success on high-stakes tests, and a requirement for twenty-first century careers.

Because of the widespread use of computerized reading development methods and computerized eye-movement recording techniques, it is likely that an increasing amount of attention will be focused on incorporating such simplified computerized techniques into reading development approaches.

QUESTIONS THAT COULD ARISE
AFTER READING THIS CHAPTER

1. What are the features of the computer technology today that are designed to develop fluency in silent reading?
2. If technology is a requirement of the many subliminal skills for developing fluency in silent reading by virtue of the many subskills that function three to five times per second, why is technology not part of each child's reading curriculum today?
3. To what extent could reading development technology also be helpful to proficient readers who read very slowly, in addition to struggling readers?

REFERENCES

Gelzer, A., & Santore, N. J. (1968). A comparison of various reading input approaches. *Journal of Educational Research, 61*(6), 267–272.

Rasinski, T., Samuels, S. J., Hiebert, E., Petscher, Y., & Feller, K. (2011). The relationship between a silent reading fluency instructional protocol on students' reading comprehension and achievement in an urban school setting. *Reading Psychology, 32*(1), 75–97.

Robinson, F. P. (1934). The tachistoscope as a measure of reading perception. *American Journal of Psychology, 46,* 123–35.

Taylor, E. A. (1957). The spans: Perception, apprehension and recognition. *American Journal of Opthalmology, 44,* 501–507.

Taylor, S. E. (1960). *Eye movement photography with the Reading Eye* (2nd ed.), 66, appendix. Huntington, NY: Educational Development Laboratories.

Taylor, S. E. (2008). *Research, rationale, and results.* Huntington Station, NY: Taylor Associates/Communications, Inc.

Taylor, S. E. (2010). *Reading Plus®.* Winooski, VT: Taylor Associates/Communications, Inc.

Volkmann, A. W. (1859). Das Tachistoskop, ein Instrument, Welches bei Untersuchung des Momentanen Sehens den Gebrauch de Elektrischens Funkens Ersetzt. Berichte Uber die Verhandlungen der Koniglich Sachischen Gesellschaft der Wissenschaften Zu Leipzig (Math. Phys. Classe) 90–98 (As given by Cassie Spencer Payne).

Chapter 4

OCULOMOTOR ACTIVITY DURING READING

Stanford E. Taylor and S. Jay Samuels

This chapter will review the visual/perceptual process that comprises a reader's oculomotor activity, which initiates the act of reading. During reading, a reader's eyes make rapid movements across a line of print, referred to as saccades (from the French word meaning "jerk" or "jolt" as on a set of reins), to fixate or execute eye pauses. Eye movements are essential in normal reading according to Javal (1879). These saccades may be in a forward or reverse manner and may fall within the word being viewed or progress to other words.

During reading, a reader's relatively habitual oculomotor activity brings print impressions to short-term memory to process as words and phrases, and to initiate comprehension of what is being read. Most people have experienced instances during reading when their minds wandered. They suddenly realized that their eyes had continued to move across lines of print, had dropped down to new lines of print, and perhaps covered complete paragraphs, while they were thinking of something else. This is a reader's usual, habitual oculomotor activity in operation. This oculomotor activity becomes largely habitual by grade 4 and was formed by the learning-to-read experiences in grades 1 through 3 as a child learns to decode, recognize words, read simple sentences, engage in oral reading, and listen to others read aloud while following along. This oculomotor activity is a result of a reader's vision, visual/functional competence (binocular coordination, ocular motility, and accuracy in tracking), perceptual accuracy (realizing the orthography of words and visual memory), and information processing (rate and sequence of word input into short-term memory). Through largely trial-and-error approaches in learning to read, a reader fashions his or her basic oculomo-

79

tor activity. The accuracy, rate, and sequence of this word intake prompted by a student's oculomotor activity directly influences ultimate comprehension. This activity will become more efficient over time as reading experience grows, but for most people their oculomotor activity rarely becomes a truly efficient process that will serve the mind well until they are able to read consistently above 300–400 words per minute.

In this chapter, the evolution of a reader's characteristic oculomotor process is examined through the grades, and computer-delivered silent reading fluency training techniques are described that can improve the visual/functional, perceptual, and information processing skills that constitute a reader's oculomotor activity. There is also a review of selected studies documenting the effectiveness of such training. Finally, eye-movement recording techniques, which are easily employed today, as described in Chapter 2, are the only definitive means of examining the efficiency of the oculomotor activity during silent reading. This chapter, then, raises questions as to how to best provide computer-training techniques in combination with teacher-directed activities to ensure the development of effective, efficient, and fluent silent reading.

NATURE OF OCULOMOTOR ACTIVITY

The eyes shift position during reading, from three to five times per second. During each fixation, word parts or whole words are perceived within a rather restricted area where print is clear and distinguishable–typically only four letters to the left of the fixation point and six to eight letters to the right. While the perceptual span for a skilled reader may be 14 to 15 characters to the right of his or her fixation, the word identification span, according to Rayner (1998) and McConkie, Underwood, Zola, and Wolverton (1985), does not generally exceed seven to eight letters to the right of the fixation. Undoubtedly, clarity of vision dictates this limit for accurate word recognition, but letters, length of words, and spacing can be perceived in the parafoveal area that will influence saccadic movements. Interestingly, the asymmetry in the extent of this letter recognition span reverses when the direction of reading changes, for example, when reading Hebrew text from right to left, as cited by Hebb (1949) and Pollatsek, Bolozky, Well, and Rayner (1981).

During each fixation, a reader processes the letter configuration of the word landed upon, perhaps uses the letter or word information in the right parafoveal area to influence the next saccade (and fixation), and continues to assess word information from prior fixations to realize phrasing, syntax, and meaning.

As words are stored in short-term memory, they are realized as letter configurations and are perhaps instantly recognized. Later, possibly after one to two or more fixations (eye stops), word recognition is finally confirmed as words are fused into phrases and larger linguistic units and ultimately comprehension is achieved. See Kliegl, Nuthmann, and Engbert (2006) for a recent discussion of "eye-movement lag." If this visual input process is inaccurate, wandering in nature, and slow in providing words to short-term memory, comprehension suffers. There are legitimate interruptions of the usual oculomotor activity if one needs to look back at unfamiliar words or phrases, or to confirm information that is not well understood. Looking back at text is conscious rereading wherein the reader reverts back several words or sentences to reread. When the reread is accomplished, the reader once again launches into his or her habitual oculomotor activity.

This finding indicates that visual performance in reading is not just a matter of visual acuity (which is symmetric across the visual field), but also of attention and learned routines of perception and oculomotor control. Visualize a parallel process wherein the mind is distributing its attention between orthographic identification that determines the realization of a word, its sound properties, conscious decoding or immediate word recognition, and the ongoing linguistic process of confirming words perceived at earlier intervals and chunking them into larger linguistic units. The ideal circumstance is demonstrated by very fluent readers, wherein the oculomotor activity, as recorded by eye-movement recording, is quite regular and rhythmical, as determined by Anderson and Dearborn (1952). Their investigation suggests that the words are being processed rapidly, sequentially, and efficiently, and higher-level cognitive functions do not need to interrupt the routine oculomotor activity to any great extent as words are fused into meaning, and the reader comprehends easily what is being read. This manner of reading is very evident in eye-movement recordings of individuals reading at more advanced and unusual levels, perhaps 500–600 words per minute.

There are still considerable variations of opinion as to what influences oculomotor activity when students are reading relatively independent, easy-to-read level content. Radach, Reilly, and Inhoff (2007) emphasized that "eye movements are not just an indication of cognition, they are part and parcel of visual processing in reading." Studies by Yang and McConkie (2001), Levy-Schoen and O'Regan (1979), and Yang (2006) suggested little cognitive control on saccadic activity; whereas other researchers, such as Rayner (1998), preferred the view that cognition exerts considerable influence on the oculomotor process. However, it is the conclusion of the authors of this chapter that the visual/functional, perceptual, and information processing skills acquired during the first three grades of learning to read exert considerable influence on the nature of the resulting oculomotor activity, with some modulating input from cognitive processes at times that can cause a reader to deviate somewhat from his or her habitual oculomotor activity at intervals. As an example, if a reader encounters an unfamiliar word and allocates processing resources to decoding that word, he or she will be encouraged to refixate, regress, and make multiple eye stops (fixations) on the target word to recognize the word accurately.

It would seem logical, then, based on all eye-movement studies to date, to acknowledge an interdependence between oculomotor activity and cognitive processes. The degree of competency in both determines reading ease and comfort, efficiency or fluency in reading, and, ultimately, comprehension.

OCULOMOTOR RESEARCH

Let us examine the findings of various researchers with regard to the nature of a reader's oculomotor activity. A saccade, or shift of fixation position, would appear to be tentatively prompted by a reader's usual or habitual oculomotor activity in terms of his or her average duration of fixation. However, this subliminal prompt to move ahead, delay movement, or regress can seemingly be modified by input from cognitive processing as suggested by Rayner (1998). Further, Festinger and Easton (1974) stated that "the efferent command for an eye movement contains information about the direction of the movement but not precise information about the velocity of the movement." What lexical or syntactic information is relayed to determine the amplitude of the saccadic movement and landing position is still being studied by many researchers.

Events Occurring During a Fixation

The following diagram depicts the events that typically occur during a beginning reader's average duration of fixation, which generally lasts approximately 330 milliseconds (ms) but can be slightly shorter or longer. Regardless of the interval of duration, these events will occur either more rapidly or in a more delayed fashion. These events involve both serial processing (events in order of occurrence) and many aspects of parallel processing (overlap of events).

Before a saccade is executed, a reader's vision is suppressed to a lower level to eliminate the blur that occurs during a saccade. Latour (1961, 1962) concluded that approximately 50 ms before the onset of an eye movement, vision is so suppressed. Gross, Vaughan, and Valenstein (1967) found that vision did not return to normal for perhaps 100–200 ms. Volkmann, Schick, and Riggs (1968), on the other hand, found that 40 ms before a saccade, vision starts to drop; that return of vision to about a 50 percent level required approximately 50 ms after executing a saccade. Ishida and Ikeda (1989) stated, "Visual sensitivity is recovered only partially at the initial part of a fixation and is recovered fully approximately 70 ms after the beginning of a fixation." Saccadic suppression slightly before and during a saccade and into the beginning of a fixation does occur or readers would see blurred print. Though the interval of suppression of vision is debated, it does exist. Further, in a study by Solan, Hansen, Shelley-Tremblay, and Ficarra (2004), students with magnocellular deficit who did not exhibit normal suppression of vision during saccadic movements did experience perceptual limitations by virtue of blurred print. Although there seems to be some difference of opinion as to how long a delay occurs before returning vision to normal, it would seem that there is some initial period during a new fixation where vision is suppressed, likely 20-30 ms minimally.

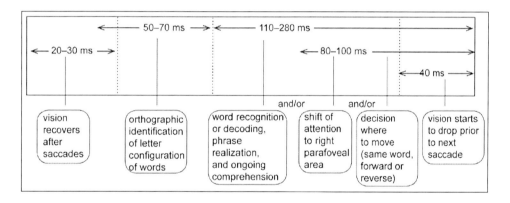

During a fixation, the perception of the orthography of a word the reader has landed upon is forwarded to short-term memory. Here, this letter configuration is stored for future recognition, or the word is recognized instantly if the word is familiar. Rayner (1998) suggested that the reader might acquire the necessary orthographic information for visual processing within the first 50–70 ms of a fixation. Following this interval of time required for accurate or inaccurate identification of the orthography of words, word recognition may occur, and attention shifts to the meaning of what has been read up to that point in time. In essence, from the moment of awareness of letter configurations, a reader engages in parallel processing, as cited by Reilly and Radach (2003, 2006) during which many aspects of word recognition and comprehension vie for attention. How much time becomes available for realizing syntax is a variable. If word recognition is instantaneous, considerable time and resources remain to associate words and to facilitate comprehension. However, if most of the time and mental effort during a fixation are required to decode or recognize a word, or if the student devotes several fixations to recognize a word, little time or capacity is left for comprehension during the average duration of fixation, according to Samuels (2006).

In the case of a more efficient and advanced reader, where the average duration of fixation (including saccade time) is likely 250 ms or less, there is considerably more parallel processing occurring, with less time spent on decoding and more time on comprehension processes. (See the following diagram.) The time for vision recovery is approximately the same, however, the time for orthographic identification will decrease to perhaps 10 ms, considering the more advanced perceptual capability of a better reader. Then the word recognition and partial phrase realization along with ongoing comprehension of what has been read to that point occurs as well as anticipation of what is to follow contextually. This time is considerably reduced in comparison to this stage for beginning readers. Sometime during this brief interval there is also a relinquishing of attention to what is being viewed and a shift of attention to the right parafoveal area that prepares the reader for the next forward saccade. Following this, vision starts to drop in preparation for the next saccade, and then the new saccade occurs.

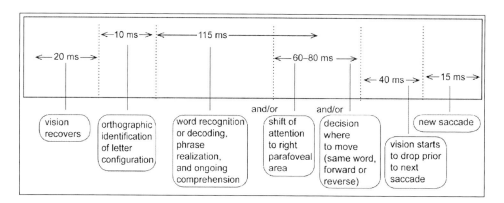

Influences on the Next Saccade

McConkie, Underwood, Zola, and Wolverton (1985) stated that the deadline for stimulus influences that could affect the amplitude of movement of the next saccade, occurs just prior to that saccade (perhaps 80–100 ms before the next saccade), which in turn determines the location of the forthcoming fixation. Radach and Kennedy (2004) stated that there is consensus in the field of reading research that, while fixating on a particular word in the foveal area where vision is the clearest, there is subliminal preprocessing of the next word to follow. Hoffman and Subramaniam (1995) also provided evidence that viso-spatial attention is required to execute a saccade, suggesting that the letter information from the parafoveal area provides some information to guide where the next saccade will land. Rayner and Morrison (1981) and others referred to this process as parafoveal pre-processing. Posner (1980) stated that "we can move attention without moving our eyes." Rayner (1998) further suggested that a relinquishing of attention is involved in generating a saccade. In essence, sufficient information must be derived from a fixation to encourage the eyes to contemplate moving on.

The exact nature of the information acquired from the parafovea is still the subject of intense research, but at this point it is clear that not only the orthography but also phonological features and morphological properties of neighboring words may be preprocessed. Some researchers claim that parafoveal information can be acquired only from one word to the right of the current fixation, while others suggest that several words may be processed within the limits of clear vision. In a landmark paper, Henderson and Ferreira (1990) showed that when the fixated word is difficult to recognize, very little parafoveal information can be acquired. Apparently, words compete for a limited pool of resources, especially when word processing is not very efficient. In addition to contributing to word recognition, letter information from the visual periphery is used to guide the eyes to the next target. McConkie and Rayner (1976) stated, "The eye is guided during reading on the basis of the peripheral vision pattern." One reasonable scenario for the process is that eye movements are planned to go to the most attractive word within the perceptual span based on clarity of vision, visuomotor constraints, and information from ongoing linguistic processing. If substantial information has been acquired from an upcoming word, it becomes a less attractive target and hence might not be fixated at all.

Regularity of Oculomotor Performance

When one studies eye-movement recordings of beginning readers, the rather erratic oculomotor performance in terms of fixations and regressions, the variations in duration of fixations, and the inaccuracy of return sweeps to new lines of print suggest that these students are attempting to employ an emerging oculomotor behavior that is not yet well refined. These erratic behaviors would seem to be largely prompted by difficulties with visual coordination, oculomotor motility, inaccuracies in tracking, difficulties in realizing the orthography of words decoding, and word recognition, as well as resulting problems with phrasing and understanding. Later, when a student has had more reading experience, likely by grade 4 or slightly higher, he or she will have developed a more regular oculomotor behavior. At these higher levels of reading competency, it seems logical to ascribe deviations from regularity of oculomotor performance more to cognitive input.

The recordings of students at various grade levels, as shown in the following display, (Taylor, 1971), suggests a general emergence of a rather regular oculomotor activity that will function better in response to the demands of comprehension.

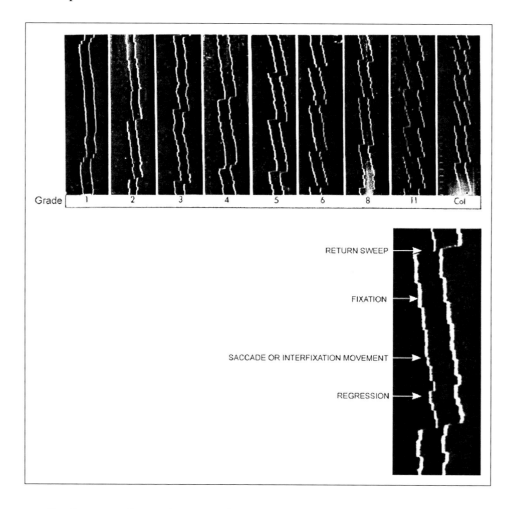

In the recordings above, each staircase of eye movement from left-to-right represents a reader's eyes moving from left-to-right across the line. The vertical length of each staircase reflects the time required to read each line of print. Note the reduction of fixations and regressions (reverse saccades) and the decrease in elapsed time (shorter staircases) to read each line of print from grade to grade.

When considering the influence cognitive processes have on the timing and movement of the eyes, one must consider whether this input occurs from the immediate word(s) being perceived or from prior fixations as the reader attends to phrasing and comprehension. Better readers will undoubtedly use the content read to predict words and thoughts to come, and this will influence, to a degree, word recognition during a fixation as well as a reader's use of parafoveal information as per McClelland and O'Regan (1981). However, departures from the usual visual input of words or oculomotor activity are often prompted one to three words later by virtue of eye-mind span, as cited by Kim, Knox, and Brown (2007) and Wagner (1999). These researchers agreed that words are visually processed ahead of cognitive processes that later confirm word recognition and assist in the realization of phrases and higher-level linguistic information.

Disparity of Movement of the Two Eyes

It is important to note that there is usually disparity in the movement (extent) amplitude of the two eyes. Heller and Radach (1999) showed that variations in amplitude between the two eyes could involve 1–1.5 letter spaces, resulting in substantial differences in the position fixated by the left versus right eye. Their suggestion that this disparity accumulates with successive fixations over a line of text has recently been confirmed by Nuthmann and Kliegl (2008), who also provided a comprehensive analysis of the large variation within and between readers. Blythe et al. (2006) reported that the disparity in fixation of the two eyes and its variability are substantially larger for children, and that differences in good readers' performance in the order of several letters were not uncommon. Some students evidence even greater disparity in the letters landed upon by the two eyes, especially visually impaired students. Any great disparity of saccade and fixation between the two eyes will certainly result in less than clear and distinct vision. The numerous reports by the College of Optometrists in Vision Development (COVD) strongly support the fact that, in reading, a student needs to be able to "aim the two eyes at the same point simultaneously and accurately" and "move the two eyes continuously as a coordinated team across the lines of print." Any difficulty in these desired binocular conditions can result only in visual discomfort as well as double, or blurry, print perception. This problem, overlooked or underestimated for decades, is now the subject of intensive research largely by the optometric community.

Skipped Words

In the oculomotor process, the eyes do not fixate on all words. Some words are skipped or passed over during saccades. Short words, high frequency and functional words, as well as words very close to an existing fixation are skipped more often. Low frequency and longer words are more likely to be landed upon. Longer words also tend to manifest more refixations and, thus, slightly longer gaze durations. A meta-analysis by Brysbaert and Vitu (1998) stated that words that "lie in the area of high visibility and/or because they are less easy to land on" are skipped. This would seem to imply that "words that lie in the area of high visibility" means that these words may be identified during a single fixation and that "less easy to land on" means a location closer than usual saccadic travel distance. Brysbaert and Vitu further stated, "on the basis of the present evidence it is beyond doubt that all comprehensive theories of word skipping should take into account the existence of involuntary word skipping due to oculomotor error," which could lead to difficulty in understanding the message of what has been read.

Amplitude of Saccadic Movement

The amplitude of saccadic movement would seem to be influenced by a reader's span of recognition, which, in turn, is bounded by limitations of vision. L. Huestegge, Radach, Corbie, and S. M. Huestegge (2008), stated that second graders make average saccades encompassing 5.27 letter spaces and that fourth graders increase the amplitude of their average saccadic excursion to 6.31 letter spaces, all seemingly within the bounds of clear vision. It is expected that more advanced readers might tend to move over a greater number of letter spaces within the bounds of the falloff of visual acuity that influences the quality of parafoveal word input. McConkie and Zola (1989) reported that college students executed average saccadic excursions of 7.2 letter spaces in terms of amplitude of excursion. Feinberg (1949) determined that seven to eight letters away from the fixation point, visual acuity drops to approximately 45 percent and rapidly diminishes beyond this distance. This is in line with the study of McConkie and Rayner (1976), which found that the average span of recognition for adults was four letters to the left of the fixation point and six to eight letters to the right, suggesting that English-speaking readers tend to pay more attention to the right area of a fixation in terms of the letters they will apprehend. (See the following illustration.)

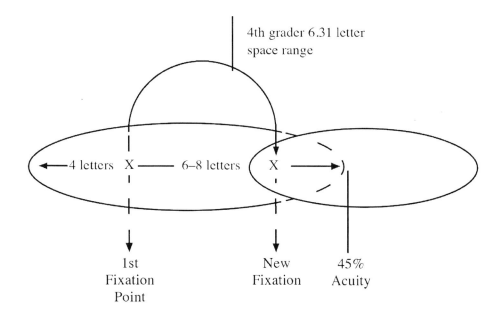

Average Span of Recognition

Interestingly, a study by Legge et al. (2007) described the relationship of visual span, as determined by limitations of vision, and resulting reading rate. This study found that the more restricted the visual span, the more fixations were required to read, resulting in a slower reading rate. This study indicated that letters that are positioned too near an acuity limit (too blurry to recognize), too close to contrast thresholds (print size), and too crowded (insufficient letter spacing) result in lower reading rates. This study concluded that, "early sensory factors do impose a bottleneck on reading speed through the mediating influence of the visual span." In essence, this explains why it is illogical to expect phrase perception during reading considering vision limitations.

Thus, it seems logical to conclude that the restriction of vision severely limits the letter clues that can be used in the right periphery. This limitation of vision will determine the extent to which letter and word information will influence the amplitude of saccadic movements as well as delineate the number of fixations employed during reading. This fact is further supported by the study by Taylor, Frackenpohl, and Pettee (1960), which reported that the average span of recognition for college students was only 1.11 words when dividing the number of fixations required for reading into the total number of words read. Interestingly, the saccadic travel distance was still only 6.3 letter spaces, similar to the findings of L. Huestegge, Radach, Corbie and S. M. Huestegge (2008), for fourth graders.

What is interesting to contemplate and study further is the extent to which a reader's background and orthographic competence affect the ability to use less distinguishable letters in the right parafoveal area productively, in terms of word recognition in a given fixation or as a stimulus for the amplitude of saccadic movement during continuous reading. It seems well accepted that oculomotor strategies and visual constraints are involved in determining fixation locations in text as put forth by Starr and Rayner (2001).

Duration of Fixation

Once a new fixation has been established, the next consideration is the length of eye pause time or duration of fixation. In general, longer, less familiar words and less predictable words tend to prompt slightly longer durations. If one looks at the overall average duration of fixation, very beginning readers tend to average around three fixations per second and intermediate through high school students tend to average about four fixations per second. According to L. Huestegge, Radach, Corbie and S. M. Huestegge (2008), gaze durations (or the total length of eye pause time based on word length and frequency of vocabulary) become less variable as readers gain experience and an expanded vocabulary. Undoubtedly, this is true if one looks at more fluent readers reading at higher rates wherein reading becomes more regular in terms of the number of fixations and duration of fixations, line-by-line, and indeed almost rhythmical, as cited by Anderson and Dearborn (1952).

Retaining Perceived Information

When considering the aspects of saccadic movements and eye pause (durations) time, there are conditions in both aspects that impinge on a reader's ability to retain what was perceived during a fixation.

Gilbert (1953) conducted some of the earliest studies that substantiated the fact that visual impressions from a given fixation can deteriorate as a result of the visual activity of moving from fixation to fixation. In this study, words were exposed tachistoscopically (flashed) in rapid sequence in the same place on a projection screen so as to require no eye movements on the part of the reader. Then similar words were presented along a line on a projection screen, requiring the reader to make a series of eye movements in order to apprehend the material.

In general, the results in Gilbert's study indicated that there was significantly less retention when eye movements were employed, as in usual reading. Further, comparison of the better readers (in the highest quartile) with the poorer readers (in the lowest quartile) indicated that the poorer readers retained substantially less when eye movements were required. These results are not difficult to understand when one considers that poorer readers will generally have more difficulty with binocular coordination and fusion, less ocular motility, and greater difficulty with tracking.

Another study by Gilbert (1959) demonstrated the effect of overlapping retinal images. In this study, groups of students were given a series of tachistoscopic exposures in which one, two, three, four, and five words were flashed. Similar exposures were made and immediately overlapped with nonsense material, causing aberration of the original word exposures.

The amount of time between the initial exposure and the overlap was gradually prolonged, and retention was checked with each increased interval. There was a substantial loss of the initial impression as a result of the superimposition of another impression. It was found that the poorer readers lost even more retention because of the overlapping images and also tended to require a greater interval of time between the word exposures and the overlapping nonsense material in order to satisfactorily stabilize, or accurately process, the visual impressions.

Thus, it is apparent that poor readers who possess less orthographic competence and visual memory will lose more from premature ocular movements, which deteriorate initial impressions.

Resulting Oculomotor Performance

It seems apparent from eye-movement recording research to date that once a relatively habitual oculomotor activity has been developed (likely by grade 4), this acquired behavior will play a dominant role in directing the eyes with periodic input, as time permits, from the parafoveal area to guide the eyes and with minimal influence in terms of contextual information if the content being read is at a student's independent reading level. When reading content approaches a student's instructional level or above, more variations will occur in the oculomotor performance by virtue of unfamiliar vocabulary and concepts, and especially in instances in which attention is redirected to the decoding of less familiar or unfamiliar words.

The consistency, or reliability, of the oculomotor activity has long been established by Eurich (1933b), Frandsen (1934), Litterer (1932), and Taylor, Frackenpohl, and Pettee (1960). These studies documented the fact that students beyond the primary level maintained a high degree of consistency of oculomotor activity in reading a given selection when the selection was on their independent, or easy-to-read, level. Further, a study by Taylor, Frackenpohl, and Pettee (1959) showed consistency of reading performance with eighth graders reading a series of selections from grade 4 to junior high level as well as college students reading a variety of high school-level selections at the same readability level. The latter study, in which interest in the various selections was also evaluated, indicated that interest did not result in significant variations in oculomotor performance.

This is not to say that the mind does not produce some variations in reading performance at intervals, but the overall performance in terms of total fixations, regressions, average duration of fixation, and reading rate tend to remain relatively consistent when subjects are reading appropriate reading level selections.

STUDIES OF OCULOMOTOR EVOLUTION IN READING

Let us examine the evolution of the oculomotor process or the changes in eye-movement behavior as reading competency develops. In a study by Taylor, Frackenpohl, and Pettee (1960), eye-movement recordings were made of more than 12,000 students in grades 1 through 12 to establish oculomotor norms. Students in the study were given a reading test selection at their grade level based on readability formulas and containing appropriate level vocabulary. The selections were 50 words in length for grades 1 to 3 and 100 words long for grades 4 and up. (See Table 4.1.)

Table 4.1

Norms			
Grade Level	1	2	3
Fixations/100 Words	224	174	155
Regressions/100 Words	52	40	35
Directional Attack %	23	23	23
Av. Span of Recognition	.45	.57	.65
Av. Duration of Fixation	.33	.30	.28
Rereading Rates (wpm)	80	115	138

Grades 1–3

The Taylor et al. study showed that grade 1 students, at mid-year, averaged 224 fixations per hundred words, or 2.24 fixations per word. (See Table 4.1.) Thus their average span of recognition was .5 of a word (total words divided by number of fixations). They averaged 52 regressions per 100 words, spending about one quarter of their time in regressions as well as additional time making recovery saccades after regressions before moving on to new words. They continued to average their usual duration of fixation, 330 ms per fixation, which was typical of their relatively habitual eye-movement behavior acquired prior to entering school, derived from general observation (Taylor and Robinson, 1963). Finally, their silent reading rate on grade-level reading content was 80 words per minute when 70 percent comprehension was achieved. With grade 1 students, oculomotor activity is quite varied and erratic in nature in terms of fixations, regressions, and duration of fixation. Keep in mind that the act of reading is not a usual human performance but one that must be learned. Beginning reading students are just learning how to stay on lines of print, move their eyes from left to right across print, and acquire a beginning reading vocabulary.

By the end of first grade, McConkie, Zola, Grimes, Kerr, and Bryant (1991) concluded that the basic oculomotor metrics of saccade positioning are fairly well developed. In essence, visual tracking is reasonably productive in terms of reading requirements. However, the oculomotor activity is still evolving.

By grade 3, students are averaging a silent reading rate of 138 words per minute. This is just inside the usual oral communication listening and speaking rate range of 125 to 175 words per minute (Taylor, 1964) that students were familiar with when they entered school. During grade 3, students will typically have reduced the number of fixations to 155 per 100 words (1.55 fixations per word or a 31 percent decrease), the number of regressions to 35. The length of the average fixation pause time, or average duration of fixation, will be reduced by reading practice to 280 ms. These developmental trends have been confirmed by more recent longitudinal studies by Radach, Schmitten, Glover, and Huestegge (2009).

Today, during the first three years of learning to read, students do not typically receive flash or tachistoscopic training in word recognition to develop automaticity (instant recognition of words within a single fixation). Flash cards are helpful in developing more rapid word recognition but do allow multiple fixations because these displays are longer than one-sixth of a second (these longer displays permit multiple fixations). As a consequence of the lack of automaticity training, students are encouraged to fixate, refixate, and regress excessively as they decode words. Keep in mind that every second of decoding promotes the use of three fixations with beginning readers, according to Taylor and Robinson (1963). In addition, oral reading that is slower than silent reading or situations in which a student is listening to slow oral reading allow an excessive number of fixations and regressions to occur (Gilbert & Gilbert, 1940, and Levy-Schoen & O'Regan, 1979).

Oral reading rates are typically considerably slower than silent reading rates. A study by Hasbrouck and Tindal (2006) cited winter oral reading rates of grade 2 students that ranged between 18–125 words correctly identified per minute (wcpm), (median 72 wcpm), and between 36–146 wcpm (median 92 wcpm) for grade 3 students. Further, a report from the Center for the Improvement of Early Reading Achievement cited Norm reading rates for oral reading as low as 60 wcpm for grade 1, 90–100 wcpm for grade 2, and 114 wcpm for grade 3. Another research report, the Oral Reading Fluency Normative Performance Chart (2000–2001) from Edformation, Inc., an educational data-gathering company, cited oral reading fluency standards for the winter period as shown in Table 4.2. Winter rates are cited in order to compare oral reading rates with the Normative silent reading rates as determined by Taylor et al. (1960), which were also secured during winter months, e.g., 80 wpm for grade 1, 115 wpm for grade 2, and 138 wpm for grade 3. (See Table 4.2.)

While oral reading practice is certainly a recommended procedure that, among other benefits, will encourage students to realize phrases in reading, silent reading practice at higher than usual oral reading rates (more in line

Table 4.2

Oral Reading Fluency Standards (Winter Period)		
Grade 1	50th%	21 wcpm
	90th%	60 wcpm
Grade 2	50th%	49 wcpm
	90th%	95 wcpm
Grade 3	50th%	73 wcpm
	90th%	125 wcpm

with a student's usual listening and speaking rates) will increase comprehension as well as improve reading rate.

During grades 1–3, the greatest developmental change in oculomotor activity occurs as students begin to acquire an adequate reading vocabulary and become more and more visually and perceptually adjusted to silent reading. However, the resulting oculomotor activity in silent reading is not typically an efficient process if one were to compare it with the oculomotor efficiency of students who have received fluency development training. For better or worse, the result of these three years of learning to read will be a relatively habitual and usually an inefficient oculomotor activity. An examination of typical eye-movement recordings of students in grades 1–3, as depicted in the first three columns of the visual on page 96, displays a reduction in the number of fixations per line of print, fewer regressions per line, some reduction in the variation of fixation duration, and an increase in reading rate while reading independent reading level content with acceptable comprehension. By contrast, the recording displayed in the last column demonstrates the performance of a third grader who has received fluency in silent reading training.

Grades 4–12

Students in grades 4 through 12 will continue to refine their oculomotor activity as shown in the following Norm Chart (Taylor et al., 1960). (See Table 4.3.)

Table 4.3

Norms									
Grade Level	4	5	6	7	8	9	10	11	12
Fixations/100 Words	139	129	120	114	109	105	101	96	94
Regressions/100 Words	31	28	25	23	21	20	19	18	17
Directional Attack %	24	22	21	20	19	19	19	19	18
Av. Span of Recognition	.72	.78	.83	.88	.92	.95	.99	1.04	1.06
Av. Duration of Fixation	.27	.27	.27	.27	.27	.27	.26	.26	.25
Rereading Rates (wpm)	158	173	185	195	204	214	224	237	250

Visagraph® Eye-Movement Recordings

Grade 1	Grade 2	Grade 3	Grade 3 (after fluency training)
Fixation: 240	Fixation: 174	Fixation: 160	Fixation: 126
Regression: 47	Regression: 32	Regression: 16	Regression: 12
Avg. Duration: .28 sec.	Avg. Duration: .28 sec.	Avg. Duration: .26 sec.	Avg. Duration: .25 sec.
Reading Rate: 91	Reading Rate: 125	Reading Rate: 143	Reading Rate: 187
Dir. Attack Difficulty: 20%	Dir. Attack Difficulty: 18%	Dir. Attack Difficulty: 8%	Dir. Attack Difficulty: 13%
Grade Level Efficiency: 1.1	Grade Level Efficiency: 2.4	Grade Level Efficiency: 3.5	Grade Level Efficiency: 6.3

Visagraph® recordings of grades 1-3 students and grade 3 student after fluency training.

Reading rates improve modestly from 158 wpm to 250 wpm by grade 12, averaging only a 10 wpm rate improvement per grade level. Fixations will drop from 139 in grade 4 to 97 in grade 12 (only an average drop of five fixations per grade level). Average span of recognition still ranges under one word up to grades 11 and 12. Regressions will drop from 31 to 17, an average drop of only one to three regressive fixations per grade level. Duration remains a constant 270 ms through grade 9 and then drops modestly to 250 ms. Thus, the principal change in reading rates results from a mild reduction of fixations and regressions. If, however, one were to compare the typical fourth grader with a fourth grader who had received fluency development training, the contrast in efficiency is quite startling as shown in the following Norm Chart (Taylor et al., 1960). (See Table 4.4.)

Table 4.4

Eye-Movement Data		
	Average Fourth Grader	Trained Fourth Grader
Fixations	139	97
Regressions	31	18
Span of Recognition	.72	1.04
Duration of Fixation	.27 ms	.26 ms
Rereading Rates	158 wpm	237 wpm

Fluency Development

Computerized reading fluency techniques can easily be used today for improvement of a student's visual, perceptual, and information processing functions, which result in more efficient oculomotor activity. Rather than leave these processes to trial-and-error evolution, specific silent reading fluency training techniques can be employed to accelerate the development of improved reading performance efficiency toward the goal of greater ease and comfort, more rapid reading, and improved comprehension.

At this point, it is important to clarify that fluency development in silent reading is not the simple task of training eye movements or simply increasing reading rate. The oculomotor control, reading rate, and comprehension advances that occur through such training result from visual/functional improvement, which affects attention, ease and comfort in reading and print clarity, greater automaticity in word recognition, more rapid word association, expanded reading vocabulary, and the development of greater competency in the use of a wide variety of comprehension skills. As mentioned previously, as a reader becomes more fluent and rapid in his or her reading, the oculomotor activity becomes more regular as the eyes and the mind work in better concert toward high reading rates and more thorough comprehension.

A multitude of eye-movement studies have investigated the extent to which word familiarity and contextual difficulty influence duration of fixation, number of fixations and re-fixations, regressions, the amplitude of saccadic excursions, and location points for forward saccades. See Van Gompel, Fischer, Murray, and Hill (2003) and Hyona, Radach, and Deubel (2003) for a recent overview. Undoubtedly, linguistic processes do impinge on oculomotor activity to a degree, but the important fact to realize is that, as a reader becomes more fluent and rapid in reading, the fewer variations there are in oculomotor behavior.

Although not totally definitive, a classroom teacher could look at the symptoms listed below that might suggest poor visual/functional, perceptual, and information processing skills that will then result in poor oculomotor performance:

- Inability to focus and sustain attention
- Evidence of visual discomfort during reading (excessive blinking, drawing close to print, tilting the head)
- Reports of print looking muddy, blurred, or doubled
- Instability in recognizing letter and letter order in words and poor visual memory
- Very slow reading rate accompanied by poor comprehension
- Excessive rereading

The ultimate conclusion, if these symptoms are observed, is that a silent reading fluency training program is needed to improve the subliminal visual/functional, perceptual, and information processing skills if the eyes and mind are to work efficiently together, resulting in improved rate of reading and better comprehension. Several computer-training techniques that have been found to be very effective in developing fluency in silent reading are:

- Flash (tachistoscopic) training with numbers, letters, and words (as shown in the following illustration) can improve a student's realization of the orthography of words and the development of greater word recognition automaticity. During these high-speed exposures, only one fixation is possible when the exposures are 1/6th of a second or faster. Increasing the accuracy with which a student identifies letter configurations and developing more instant recognition of words within a single fixation result in more time and mental capacity for word association, phrasing, and understanding during each duration of fixation. Additionally, more effective use of parafoveal information will then be made during each fixation.

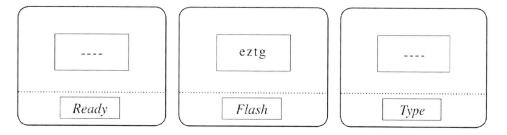

- The Guided Reading program,[1] through timed left-to-right displays of print (in the manner shown in the following example where a moving window displays print) can result in a number of changes that will produce improved reading efficiency in both oculomotor behaviors and cognitive functions.

the   largest   car-racing

The scanning training provided by these left-to-right timed displays of text will have a number of beneficial results. As students read and model their reading behavior in accord with such text displays, the following changes occur.

- Visual functioning (binocular coordination), ocular motility (the ability to move the eyes instead of the head), and accuracy in tracking (both horizontally and vertically) improve.
- The faster-than-usual occluding of print from left-to-right discourages habitual regressions and also eliminates recovery eye movements

---

1. In this chapter and in subsequent chapters, the term guided reading will be used to describe a timed left-to-right display of text. This term has evolved from the use of the Guided Reader™, a device used in the 1980s to develop fluency in silent reading. Today, many educators also use the term "guided reading" to describe teacher-directed small-group reading enhancement activities.

that typically follow regressions, resulting in improved sequence of word input into short-term memory. Overall fixations are reduced as the student learns to perceive more rapidly and sequentially.

- Duration of fixation shortens as a result of the brief, timed displays of all words. Word recognition time decreases and greater automaticity will be encouraged if the reading content provides frequent repetition of high-frequency vocabulary through shorter, timed displays of each word.
- Students are encouraged to direct more of their attention to the right of their fixation point, which increases the potential for them to use parafoveal letter clues to better guide upcoming saccadic excursions.
- The left-to-right unveiling of words in a left-to-right fashion enhances the potential for orthographic awareness, and the timed closing down of word displays discourages conscious attention to decoding and encourages more rapid word recognition.
- Risk-taking in word perception is encouraged, which allows the student to proceed with continuous reading and later to confirm recognition of encountered words during phrasing and to confirm meaning through the use of the context that follows.
- Comprehension improves as students input words more rapidly and sequentially into short-term memory and as comprehension questions guide the students to more global and thorough comprehension.

In a reading development system such as Reading Plus®, flash and Guided Reading program techniques (in which timed left-to-right displays of text are employed) form the foundation for developing the visual/functional, perceptual, and information processing skills that determine a student's fluency in reading and his or her oculomotor efficiency. Beyond these forms of basic skill training, there is also essential scaffolding of instruction, starting with appraisals that ensure that each student begins training in appropriate level content. Then, based on a student's reading rate and comprehension progress, training is constantly modified in terms of level of lesson content, format and length of reading segments, modification of the rate of presentation of text, rereading as needed, and combinations of both independent and Guided Reading.

In a Miami, Florida, study in 2006, reported by Rasinski, Samuels, Hiebert, Petscher, and Feller (2011), 5,758 students in 98 schools participated in Reading Plus®. These students were compared with 10,385 nonparticipating students. Participating students had approximately 30 hours with Reading Plus®. Findings indicated that the program resulted in significant improvements in reading comprehension and overall reading achievement on a criterion-referenced reading test for grades 5, 6, 7, 8, and 9 and on a norm-referenced test of reading achievement for grades 4, 5, 6, 7, 8, and 10.

Moreover, mean gains made by students in the Reading Plus® intervention were greater than mean gains for all students at the state and district levels. In a 2006 study of second grade students by Shelley-Tremblay and Eyer (2009), evidence provided showed the impact that fluency in silent reading development techniques can have on oculomotor and perceptual development. The second grade students engaged in Reading Plus® programs for a semester, involving both flash and Guided Reading training. Table 4.5 displays the contrast between the normative performance of second graders (Taylor et al., 1960) and the performance of second graders who received a semester of fluency development training. This eye-movement data was secured at mid-year for both the normative performance and the fluency training group.

Table 4.5

Visagraph® Eye Movement Recording Data		
	Normative Performance	Following Fluency Training
Fixations	174	152 (155 is norm for 3rd graders)
Regressions	57	26 (25 is norm for 6th graders)
Reading Rate	115 wpm	150 wpm (158 wpm is norm for 4th graders)

In addition to the substantial Visagraph® changes made by second graders who received fluency training, the scores on the Gates-MacGinitie test showed that the Reading Plus® group made twice the gains of the control group on all subsections of the test.

In a study by Schlange, Patel, and Caden (1999), sixth and eighth grade students, judged to be at risk in terms of academic failure, were enrolled in a Reading Plus® program for only a two-month period. Students using Reading Plus® statistically exceeded the gain over "paired" nonparticipants on the Iowa Tests of Basic Skills (ITBS) scores. Additionally, Visagraph® eye-movement recording pre- and post-examinations revealed significant improvement in oculomotor performance in terms of a reduction in students' number of fixations, regressions, and durations of fixation, while at the same time improving their reading rates significantly. Beyond this, students who participated in Reading Plus® demonstrated considerable improvement in binocular coordination as measured in 12 different visual performance areas.

SUMMARY

All research to date, with regard to oculomotor development in authentic reading, suggests that students would profit from training in fluent silent reading if their oculomotor and comprehension processes are to become truly efficient. The development of the skills that comprise the oculomotor process cannot be left to chance development. Computer-based fluency development techniques to improve silent reading are available today and are essential in that they allow students to model their reading behavior through visual guidance and, in doing so, alter their visual, perceptual, and information processing skills–and ultimately their oculomotor activity. A teacher cannot direct the high-speed activity of silent reading in which a reader moves his or her eyes three to five times per second. Nor can a student control his or her visual and perceptual behavior. As a teacher guides students' development of reading, vocabulary, and comprehension, continued fluency in silent reading development must also be provided through computer approaches if students are to achieve their maximum silent reading potential.

RECORDING OF THE OCULOMOTOR ACTIVITY

Today, the only means of evaluating a student's oculomotor development and efficiency in reading is through eye-movement recording. The findings of the National Reading Panel (2000 report) documented that better readers make fewer fixations and regressions, employ shorter average duration of fixations, and read more rapidly. The Taylor et al. (1960) Norm Study was cited in this NRP report.

When eye-movement information about a student's reading efficiency and visual/functional and perceptual readiness for reading, as described in Chapter 2, is combined with other standardized reading and state competency tests, which are primarily reading effectiveness measurements, a more complete understanding of the overall reading proficiency of a student becomes available.

QUESTIONS THAT COULD ARISE
AFTER READING THIS CHAPTER

1. To what degree can the improvement of visual/functional, perceptual and information processes that comprise the oculomotor activity improve comprehension?

2. To what extent can oculomotor development be facilitated using today's computerized fluency development technology training?
3. Can an eye-movement evaluation of a student's oculomotor activity suggest more appropriate and instructional decisions?
4. What constitutes a truly comprehensive beginning reading curriculum for grades 1 through 3 and a supplemental reading improvement approach for grades 4 through 6?

This chapter also raises questions as how best to embrace computer technology to develop many of the high-speed processes of silent reading. While a teacher can and should continue with those instructional areas that require student/teacher interaction (such as introduction of reading vocabulary, phonics guidance, direction of reading comprehension goals and strategies, and appreciation of literary content), it would seem logical that computer technology must also be provided to students to ensure the development of the more fundamental visual/perceptual skills that function three to five times per second.

REFERENCES

Anderson, I. H., & Dearborn, W. F. (1952). *The psychology of teaching reading.* New York: Ronald Press.

Blythe, H. L., Liversedge, S. P., Joseph, H., White, S., Findlay, J. M., & Rayner, K. (2006). The binocular coordination of eye movements during reading in children and adults. *Vision Research, 46,* 3898–3909.

Brysbaert, M., & Vitu, F. (1998). Word skipping: Implications for theories of eye movement control in reading. In G. Underwood (Ed.), *Eye guidance in reading and scene perception* (pp. 125–148). Oxford, England: Elsevier.

Edformation, Inc. (2000–2001 School Year). Oral Reading Fluency Normative Performance Chart.

Eurich, A. C. (1933a). Additional data on the reliability and validity of photographic eye-movement records. *Journal of Educational Psychology, 24,* 380–84.

Eurich, A. C. (1933b). Fourth- and fifth-grade standards for photographic eye-movement records. *Journal of Genetic Psychology, 43,* 466–471.

Eurich, A. C. (1933c). The reliability and validity of photographic eye-movement records. *Journal of Educational Psychology, 24,* 118–22.

Feinberg, R. (February, 1949, March, 1949). A study of some aspects of peripheral visual acuity. *American Journal of Optometry and Archives of American Academy of Optometrics, 26,* 49–56, 105–119.

Festinger, L., & Easton, A. M. (1974). Inferences about the efferent system based on a perceptual illusion produced by eye movements. *Psychological Review,* 81, 44–58.

Fisher, D., Frey, N., & Lapp, D. (2008). *In a reading state of mind: Brain research, teacher modeling, and comprehension instruction.* Newark, DE: International Reading Association.

Frandsen, A. (1934). An eye-movement study of objective examination questions. *Genetic Psy-*

chology Monograph, 16(2), 79–138.

Gilbert, L. C. (1953). Speed of processing visual stimuli and its relation to reading. *Journal of Educational Psychology, 50,* 8–14.

Gilbert, L. C. (1959). Saccadic movements as a factor in visual perception in reading. *Journal of Educational Psychology, 50,* 15–19.

Gilbert, L. C., & Gilbert, D. W. (1940). Effect on silent reading of attempting to follow oral reading. *Elementary School Journal, 40,* 614–621.

Gross, E. G., Vaughan, Jr., H. G., & Valenstein, E. (1967). Inhibition of visual evoked responses to patterned stimuli during voluntary eye movements. *Electroencephalography and Clinical Neurophysiology, 22*(3), 204–209.

Hasbrouck, J., & Tindal, G. A. (2006). Oral reading fluency norms: A valuable assessment tool for reading teachers. *The Reading Teacher, 59,* 636–644.

Hebb, D. O. (1949). *Organization of behavior–A neuropsychological theory.* New York: John Wiley & Sons, Inc.

Heller, D., & Radach, R. (1999). Eye movements in reading: Are two eyes better than one? In W. Becker, H. Deubel, & T. Mergner (Eds.), *Current oculomotor research: Physiological and psychological aspects* (pp. 341–348). New York: Plenum Press.

Henderson, J. M., & Ferreira, F. (1990). Effects of foveal processing difficulty on the perceptual span in reading: Implications for attention and eye-movement control. *Journal of Experimental Psychology: Learning, Memory, and Cognition, 16,* 417–429.

Hoffman, J. E., & Subramaniam, B. (1995). The role of visual attention in saccadic eye movements. *Perception & Psychophysics, 57,* 787–795.

Huestegge, L., Radach, R., Corbie, D., & Huestegge, S. M. (2009). Oculomotor and Linguistic Determinants of Reading Development: A Longitudinal Study. *Vision Research, 40,* 2948–4959.

Hyona, J., Radach, R., & Deubel, H. (Eds.). (2003). *The mind's eye: Cognitive and applied aspects of eye movements.* Oxford, England: Elsevier.

Ishida, T., & Ikeda, M. (1989). Temporal properties of information extraction in reading studied by a text-mask replacement technique. *Journal of the Optical Society A: Optics and Image Science, 6,* 1624–1632.

Javal, L. E. (1879). Essai sur a physiologie de la lecture. *Annales d'Oculistique, 82,* 242–253.

Kim, K., Knox, M., & Brown, J. (2007). Eye movement and strategic reading. In Y. Goodman & P. Martens (Eds.), *Critical issues in early literacy: Research and pedagogy* (pp. 47–58). New Jersey: Lawrence Erlbaum Associates, Inc.

Kliegl, R., Nuthmann, A., & Engbert, R. (2006). Tracking the mind during reading: The influence of past, present, and future words on fixation durations. *Journal of Experimental Psychology: General, 135,* 12–35.

LaTour, P. L. (1961). The eye and its timing. *Report of the Institute for Perception,* 121.

LaTour, P. L. (1962). Visual threshold during eye movements. *Vision Research, 2,* 261–262.

Legge, G. E., Cheung, S.-H., Yu, D., Chung, S. T. L., Lee, H.-W., & Owens, D. P. (2007). The case for the visual span as a sensory bottleneck in reading. *Journal of Vision, 7*(2):9, 1–15.

Levy-Schoen, A., & O'Regan, J. K. (1979). The control of eye movements in reading. In P. A. Kilers, M. E. Wrolstad, & H. Bouma (Eds.), *Processing of visible language* (pp. 7–36). New York: Plenum Press.

Litterer, O. F. (1932). An experimental analysis of reading performance. *Journal of Experimental Education, 1,* 28–37.

McClelland, J. L., & O'Regan, J. K. (1981). Expectations increase the benefit derived from parafoveal visual information in reading words aloud. *Journal of Experimental Psychology: Human Perception and Performance, 7*(3), 634–644.

McConkie, G. W., & Rayner, K. (1976). Asymmetry of the perceptual span in reading. *Bulletin of the Psychonomic Society, 8,* 365–368.

McConkie, G. W., Underwood, N. R., Zola, D., & Wolverton, G. S. (1985). Some temporal characteristics of processing during reading. *Journal of Experimental Psychology: Human Perception and Performance, 11,* 168–186.

McConkie, G. W., & Zola, D. (1989). Some characteristics of readers' eye movements. In C. von Euler, I. Lundberg, I., & G. Lennerstrand (Eds.), *Brain and reading* (pp. 369–381). London: Macmillan Press.

McConkie, G. W., Zola, D., Grimes, J., Kerr, P. W., & Bryant, N. R. (1991). Children's eye movements during reading. In J. F. Stein (Ed.), *Vision and visual dyslexia* (pp. 251–262). London: Macmillan.

National Institute of Child Health and Human Development. (2000). *Report of the National Reading Panel. Teaching children to read: An evidence-based assessment of the scientific research literature on reading and its implications for reading instruction: Report of the subgroups* (NIH Publication No. 00–4769). Washington, DC: U. S. Government Printing Office.

Nuthmann, A., & Kliegl, R. (2008). An examination of binocular reading fixations based on sentence corpus data. *Journal of Vision, 9*(5): 31, 1–28.

Pollatsek, A., Bolozky, S., Well, A. D., & Rayner, K. (1981) Asymmetries in the perceptual span for Israeli readers. *Brain and Language, 14*(1), 174–80.

Posner, M. I. (1980). Orienting of attention. *Quarterly Journal of Experimental Psychology, 32,* 3–25.

Radach, R., & Heller, D. (1995). Binocular coordination in complex visual tasks. *Perception, 24,* 72.

Radach, R., & Kennedy, A. (2004). Theoretical perspectives on eye movements in reading: Past controversies, current issues, and an agenda for future research. *European Journal of Cognitive Psychology, 16,* 3–26.

Radach, R., Reilly, R., & Inhoff, A. W. (2007). Models of oculomotor control in reading: Towards a theoretical foundation of current debates. In R. van Gompel, M. Fischer, W. Murray, & R. Hill (Eds.), *Eye movements: A window on mind and brain* (pp. 237–270). Oxford, England: Elsevier.

Radach, R., Schmitten, C., Glover, L., & Huestegge, L. (2009). How children read for comprehension: Eye movements in developing readers. In R. K. Wagner, C. Schatschneider, & C. Phythian-Sence (Eds.), *Beyond decoding: Behavioral and biological foundations of reading comprehension* (pp. 75–106). New York: Guilford.

Rasinski, T., Samuels, S. J., Hiebert, E., Petscher, Y., & Feller, K. (2011). The relationship between a silent reading fluency instructional protocol on students' reading comprehension and achievement in an urban school setting. *Reading Psychology, 32*(1), 75–97.

Rayner, K. (1998). Eye movements in reading and information processing: 20 years of research. *Psychological Bulletin, 124,* 372–422.

Rayner, K., & Morrison, R. (1981). Eye movements and identifying words in parafoveal vision. *Bulletin of the Psychonomic Society, 17,* 135–138.

Reilly, R., & Radach, R. (2003). Foundations of an interactive activation model of eye movement control in reading. In J. Hyona, R. Radach, & H. Deubel (Eds.), *The mind's eye: Cognitive and applied aspects of eye movement research* (pp. 429–455). Oxford, England: Elsevier.

Reilly, R., & Radach, R. (2006). Some empirical tests of an interactive activation model of eye movement control in reading. *Cognitive Systems Research, 7,* 34–55.

Samuels, S. J. (2006). Toward a model of reading fluency. In S. J. Samuels & A. E. Farstrup (Eds.), *What research has to say about fluency instruction* (pp. 24–46). Newark, DE: International Reading Association.

Schlange, D., Patel, H., & Caden, B. (1999). Evaluation of the Reading Plus 2000 and Visagraph System as a remedial program for academically "at risk" sixth and eighth grade students: A pilot study. *Optometry and Vision Science 76,* poster 11.

Shelley-Tremblay, J., & Eyer, J. (2009). Effect of the Reading Plus program on reading skills in second graders. *Journal of Behavioral Optometry, 20*(3), 59–66.

Solan, H. A., Hansen, P., Shelley-Tremblay, J., & Ficarra, A. (2004). M-cell deficit and reading disability: A preliminary study of the effects of temporal vision-processing therapy. *Optometry, 75,* 640–650.

Starr, M. S., & Rayner, K. (2001). Eye movements during reading: Some current controversies. *Trends in Cognitive Sciences, 5,* 156–163.

Taylor, S. E. (1964). *Listening. What research says to the teacher, 29.* Washington, DC: National Education Association.

Taylor, S. E. (1971). The dynamic activity of reading. *EDL Research and Information Bulletin (9):* 48. New York: EDL/McGraw Hill.

Taylor, S. E., Frackenpohl, H., & Pettee, J. L. (1959). A report on two studies of the validity of eye-movement photography as a measurement of reading performance. *Reading in a Changing Society, International Reading Association Conference Proceeding, 4.*

Taylor, S. E., Frackenpohl, H., & Pettee, J. L. (1960). Grade level norms for the components of the fundamental reading skill. *EDL Research and Information Bulletin, 3.* New York: EDL/McGraw Hill.

Taylor, S. E., & Robinson, H. A. (1963, February). The relationship of the oculomotor efficiency of the beginning reader to his success in learning to read. Paper presented at the meeting of the American Educational Research Association, Chicago, IL.

Van Gompel, M., Fischer, W., Murray, W., & Hill, R. (Eds.). (2003). *Eye movements: A window on mind and brain.* Oxford, England: Elsevier.

Volkmann, F. C. (1962). Vision during voluntary saccadic eye movements. *Journal of the Optical Society of America, 52,* 571–578.

Volkmann, F. C., Schick, A. M., & Riggs, L. A. (1968). Time course of visual inhibition during voluntary saccades. *Journal of the Optical Society of America, 58*(4), 562–569.

Wagner, R. K. (1999). From simple structure to complex function: Major trends in the development of theories, models, and measurements of memory. In G. R. Lyon & N. A. Krasnegor (Eds.), *Attention, memory, and executive function* (2nd printing, pp. 139–156). Baltimore: Paul H. Brookes Publishing Co.

Yang, S. N. (2006). An oculomotor-based model of eye movements in reading: The competition/interaction model. *Cognitive Systems Research, 7,* 56–69.

Yang, S. N., & McConkie, G. W. (2001). Eye movements during reading: A theory of saccade initiation times. *Vision Research, 41,* 3567–3585.

Chapter 5

MOVING TOWARD FLUENCY IN SILENT READING

STANFORD E. TAYLOR AND TIMOTHY RASINSKI

This chapter explores fluency in both oral and silent reading and describes the possible results of an overemphasis on oral reading on silent reading performance. The visual/functional, perceptual, and information processing skills that comprise fluency in silent reading are explained, as well as the need for vocabulary and comprehension reinforcement, all factors necessary to attaining meaningful levels of fluency in silent reading.

Fluency in reading is widely recognized as a critical need for reading competency. Fluency in both oral reading and silent reading should certainly be desired goals of our educational practices today. Fluency in reading is stressed in the "No Child Left Behind" legislation, in the Report of the National Reading Panel (2000), and in numerous research reports by the journal, *Scientific Studies of Reading* (2001). In this journal Kame'enui and Simmons (2001) stated, "Clearly, the ability to read accurately and rapidly is so fundamental in reading success that it just has to be right." Further, the National Reading Panel (2000) found that 44 percent of a national representative sampling of fourth grade students were found to be disfluent. The National Reading Panel concluded, "Children who do not develop reading fluency, no matter how bright they are, will continue to read slowly and with great effort." Stahl and Kuhn (2000) in a Center for the Improvement of Early Reading Achievement report stated, "If children fail to make the transition to fluent reading, they will encounter significant difficulties in constructing meaning from the text." Reutzel and Hollingsworth (1993) reinforced the need for fluency development: "The development of reading fluency has been a neglected part of reading instruction despite the fact that many reading authorities consider it to be an important part of the reading curriculum." Rasinski (2006)

107

further notes: "The link between fluency and overall reading proficiency is now well established. Nevertheless, our understanding of reading fluency and its place in the reading process and reading curriculum is far from complete."

When addressing the need for fluency development, it is important to realize that oral reading fluency and silent reading fluency employ many of the same skills and share some, but not all, the same goals.

A widely held definition of oral reading fluency is the ability to read with accurate word pronunciation, at a reasonable rate, and with proper phrasing (prosody) that reflects a meaningful interpretation of the text. Oral reading is usually, and most authentically, done for the purpose of communicating meaning to a listening audience. A slightly different definition of fluency in silent reading is the ability to read with sustained attention and concentration, ease and comfort, at adequate silent reading rates (for various grade levels), and with good comprehension by the reader. Comprehension, in various forms, should be the key goal of both oral and silent reading.

One is then led to ask these questions. What is the role of oral reading practices in developing fluency? What are the differences between oral and silent reading? What are the effects of oral reading practices on silent reading behavior? What factors permit sustained attention and ease and comfort in reading? What factors permit adequate reading rates to be achieved? What are adequate silent reading rates? What factors contribute to thorough understanding and meaningful comprehension? This chapter, then, attempts to answer these questions.

ORAL READING/REPEAT ORAL READING OUTCOMES

Fluency in oral reading is widely embraced as a key goal in the primary grades as well as repeat oral reading as a means of developing such fluency. Certainly, expressive oral reading can help very early readers realize how printed words are translated into meaningful oral language. However, there are pitfalls in overstressing oral reading that must be understood. There must be a balance between oral reading practice and silent reading practice if silent reading proficiency is to be attained. While oral and silent reading employ many of the same skills of reading, there are pronounced differences that must be considered as well as the effect of oral reading on silent reading behavior.

Oculomotor Behavior

While a thorough discussion of oculomotor activity is contained in Chapter 4, it is first essential to understand that beginning readers, when they enter school, do exert an already formed and relatively habitual oculomotor (eye-movement) behavior. S. E. Taylor and Robinson (1963) revealed that kindergarten and first graders typically move their eyes three times per second in most visual tasks, a relatively habitual oculomotor activity conditioned by preschool observation activities in general. They then carry this habit of frequently moving their eyes into reading. However, beginning readers cannot typically identify and recognize words in their usual eye-pause time of .33 seconds and so they resort to making multiple fixations (eye-stops) to recognize words. First graders make an average of 2.2 fixations per word during silent reading as determined in the extensive norm study of oculomotor behavior in silent reading by S. E. Taylor, Frackenpohl, and Pettee (1960). Since oral reading is typically slower than usual silent reading, oral reading may condition excessive visual wandering with more fixations per word. This can result in a habitual inefficient oculomotor silent reading activity by the intermediate grades.

It has long been established by such researchers as Gilbert (1959), who, using eye-movement recording techniques, documented the detrimental effect of slow or nonfluent oral reading on the visual intake process of better readers as they listened to poorer readers read aloud. Better readers nearly doubled the number of fixations (eye-stops) and regressions (reverse eye-movements) while listening to poorer readers read aloud. A poorer oral reader, who is slow in recognizing words, will likewise employ considerable visual wandering when reading aloud. As a result, Gilbert recommended that oral reading, though helpful to the teacher in evaluating word recognition, be limited. Gilbert pointed out that poor oral reading can condition a poor oculomotor behavior and that this cannot benefit children learning to read. "Reading to pronounce, even for skilled readers, increases the number and duration of fixations," according to Hendricks and Kolk (1997).

In a recent Web-based review of research with regard to oral reading by Thompson and Gickling (1992), the statement was made that, "The data are unmistakable in condemning the routine practice of requiring silent readers to follow the oral reading of poor or mediocre students." Smith (1973) stated also, "Even the oral reading of excellent students is questionable because the eye movements of the best oral readers are undesirable for a silent reader."

Recently, eye-movement recording data of some (not all) students' performances in both oral reading and silent reading showed a loss of binocular coordination and accuracy in visual tracking when they read aloud, as contrasted with their visual performance when reading silently. The sample Visagraph® recordings, depicted in the following examples, show one reader's difference in visual performance when reading orally versus silently.

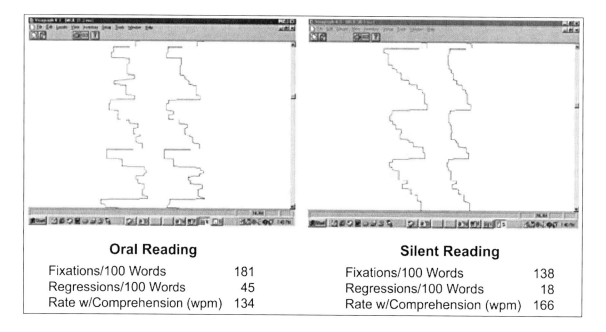

Oral Reading		**Silent Reading**	
Fixations/100 Words	181	Fixations/100 Words	138
Regressions/100 Words	45	Regressions/100 Words	18
Rate w/Comprehension (wpm)	134	Rate w/Comprehension (wpm)	166

Not only are a greater number of fixations and regressions typically employed during oral reading, but also the process of "seeing and saying" with some students seems to disturb the oculomotor process and decrease the efficiency of their binocular coordination and accuracy in tracking. These findings strongly suggest the need for more eye-movement research in conjunction with oral reading practices at various levels of proficiency. It is very likely that overstressing oral reading without a proper balance of silent reading practice can result in inefficient oculomotor development, which then inhibits fluency in silent reading.

Rate of Reading

Reading rate is the area of greatest confusion and lack of agreement. For perspective, it is essential to understand that the usual speaking and listening rates for beginning readers range between 125–175 wpm, according to S. E. Taylor (1964). The stated goal of most reports related to oral rereading is for students to read expressively in a proper prosodic manner at what is termed fluent oral reading rates. But what are fluent oral rates? A recent research report by Kame'euni and Simmons (2001) stated "A first grader orally reading a grade level passage at the uncommon rate of 90 wpm is an awesome sight." As stated in Chapter 4, Hasbrouck and Tindal (2006) cited final oral reading rates of grade 2 students that ranged between 78–106 wpm and grade 3 students between 93–123 wpm. A report from the Center for the Improvement of Early Reading Achievement cited norm reading rates for oral reading as low as 60 wpm for grade 1, 90–100 wpm for grade 2, and 114 wpm for grade 3. Another research report from Edformation, Inc., (2000–2001) an educational data-gathering company, cited oral reading fluency standards for the winter period as shown below. (Winter rates were selected in order to compare oral reading rates with the normative silent reading rates by S. E. Taylor et al. (1960), which were also secured during winter months. The silent reading rates were 80 wpm for grade 1, 115 wpm for grade 2, and 138 wpm in grade 3.)

- Grade 1: 50th%–21 wpm; 90th%–60 wpm
- Grade 2: 50th%–49 wpm; 90th%–95 wpm
- Grade 3: 50th%–73 wpm; 90th%–125 wpm

Additionally, S. E. Taylor (1976), in a study with 2,742 grade 1, 2, and 3 students, found that grade 1 students rereading previously read and familiar basal reading content aloud achieved median reading rates of only 90 wpm. Median aural rate was 105 wpm for grade 2 students and 125 wpm for grade 3 students.

Even the higher than usual oral reading rate of 90 words per minute for grade 1 students is still very slow when compared with usual oral communication and does encourage students to average two fixations (eye-stops) for every word. The lower cited rate of 60 words per minute would encourage three or more fixations per word. One is then led to question the low rate goals to be achieved by oral reading and their transfer to silent reading performances.

Buswell (1922) reported a speed of 250 words per minute with older students reading aloud as compared to up to 600 words per minute during silent reading. See Juel and Holmes (1981) and Salasoo (1986) for additional investigations.

For perspective, a study to develop higher levels of silent reading by S. E. Taylor (1976–1978) involving 3,142 primary grade students showed that fluency development training involving left and right projection of basal content, reading along while listening to basal recordings at student-selected audio rates, and "flash" training (rapid timed exposures) of basal vocabulary, led to grade 1 students achieving median silent reading rates of 146 wpm (S.D. ranging from 120 wpm to 194 wpm) and grade 2 students achieving median silent reading rates of 162 wpm (S.D. ranging from 128 wpm and 207 wpm). One is led to consider whether attaining high rates should be a goal of oral reading. Would it not be more reasonable to focus on prosodic delivery in oral reading, which reflects the meaning of the passage read?

Vocalization

During oral reading there is necessarily an emphasis on vocalizing, and this cannot help but result in a carryover to some increase in vocalization during silent reading, which will limit silent reading rates and, ultimately, comprehension. In silent reading, some students vocalize to reinforce word recognition (a form of word recognition rehearsal). But saying words during oral or silent reading slows down the reading process and can become habitual and overly depended upon if overemphasized.

Most educators agree that vocalization should be discouraged during silent reading if reasonable silent reading rate goals are to be acquired and good comprehension is to be achieved. As a consequence, teachers, over the years, have been employing techniques to discourage vocalizing during silent reading in order to achieve reasonable rates of reading and good comprehension.

It is likely that overstressing oral reading and oral rereading practice will encourage more vocalization that may carry over into a student's silent reading behavior. Consequently, more study needs to be devoted to the transfer of vocalization from oral reading into silent reading.

Comprehension

During oral reading and repeat reading, attention must necessarily be primarily focused on perceiving and recognizing words (visual input process) and producing acceptable oral expression (prosody).

Pronouncing aloud what is read during oral reading when the goal is word perfect pronunciation lessens attention to understanding. Many teachers have had the experience of listening to a child read aloud and then when a sentence is finished, noting his or her lack of ability to recall the meaning of what was just read. Attention had been totally devoted to word recognition and pronunciation. As a result, comprehension suffered.

As noted previously, oral reading does require additional time to pronounce the words in an acceptable, expressive manner in contrast to the time that would be required to read in silent reading. During this additional time, many extra fixations (eye-stops) and regressions (reverse eye-movements) will occur. This additional time will tend to encourage a "wandering" oculomotor (visual intake) activity. As a result, short-term memory may be overtaxed by virtue of the longer time required to "receive the message," the correcting of out-of-order sequences of word impressions caused by visual wandering to attain proper syntax. This lack of sequence of word input into short-term memory can limit a student's ability to "chunk" word impressions into large syntactical units such as phrases. When short-term memory is overtaxed, literal comprehension is diminished.

Consider also that expressive oral reading requires that a student employ an eye voice span (distance from the word being pronounced and the fixation point of the reader) of about 1.5 to 3 words according to Buswell (1922). This means words must be stored in short-term memory accurately and remembered well (visual memory) as oral expression takes place or the oral reader will be encouraged to make many regressions during oral expression to double check what was originally perceived. Any such excessive regressions will continue to create a visual "wandering" approach to reading that may prove detrimental to perception and understanding.

In summary, reading practices that encourage excess fixations and regressions can also encourage the development of a habitual inefficient oculomotor activity that later will diminish comprehension in silent reading.

Interest

The process of rereading previously read content orally would not appear to be a very stimulating task for children. Even when they understand that the goal of rereading is to read more automatically with good expression, this practice may not be very interesting as is the case in current and popular reading fluency programs where the goal of the rereading is increased reading speed with minimal regard for expression or meaning. Rasinski (1990), in his study of "Effects of Repeated Reading and Listening while Reading," commented, "Repeated reading may have several practical drawbacks; over the long term students may tire from its use. Students may lose interest in, and motivation for, the repetition of previously read material." Rasinski, Samuels, Hiebert, Petscher, and Feller (2011) note that an alternative to this practice is authentic oral rehearsal of reading material that is meant for an eventual performance for a listening audience. Materials such as poetry and readers theater scripts are well suited for such activities. Alternatively, new content that repeats high-frequency core vocabulary may also serve the same purpose of repeated reading and be of higher interest to readers.

Transfer

Lastly, there is the question of the transfer of repeat oral reading practice to both fluency in reading new content orally and to silent reading. Stahl and Kuhn (2002) found, "Repeated reading did not seem to make an impact on children's oral reading or comprehension." Rashotte and Torgesen (1985) stated, "If stories have few shared words, repeat reading is not more effective for improving reading speed than an equivalent amount of nonrepeated reading." Thus far the aspect of transfer of fluency to the reading of new content to be read orally and to silent reading has not been adequately demonstrated. Conversely, a considerable body of research has shown that repeated oral reading of common reading materials does lead to positive improvements in students' reading achievement (Rasinski, Reutzel, Chard, and Linan, 2011).

However, there is more to consider beyond what might be acceptable in terms of oral fluency when considering transfer to silent reading. In silent reading, much higher levels of automaticity of word recognition are required (perhaps only .10 sec. or less to perceive a word out of the usual eye-pause time of .33 sec.) leaving more time to devote to comprehension. Additionally, much less visual wandering and more sequential realization of syntax at higher rates of association, reduced vocalization, and increased levels of visual/functional competence (binocular coordination, oculomotility, and accuracy of tracking or directional attack) are requisites.

Writing for The Center for the Improvement of Early Rereading, Stahl and Kuhn (2000) stated, "There are many unanswered questions. What the role of repetitive reading is and whether increasing the amount of reading would have similar effects." This report questioned the various kinds of practices employed or those that might be employed. "We know that the time spent reading is an important variable in learning to read, but time spent reading what? Is reading difficult material more useful than reading easy material? Is reading the same material more useful than reading new material? Are there different effects for oral and silent reading" (pp. 65–66)?

It would seem logical that one of the primary goals of employing oral rereading practice would be to ensure that primary grade students will be able to read silently in a more fluent manner. With this in mind, would it not be logical to schedule silent reading practice after oral reading practice to help students capitalize on the word association and prosody developed in oral reading as students read silently? Further, the higher rates of usual silent reading will assist comprehension, which, after all, is the ultimate goal of reading.

Appraisal Considerations

The principal outcomes of using oral reading as an appraisal technique would seem to judge rate and accuracy of word recognition, realization of syntax, and acceptable prosodic delivery. By contrast, a more definitive measurement of the process of silent reading can only be made using eye-movement recording techniques that allow an evaluation of the underlying oculomotor, visual, perceptual, and information processing, which constitute a student's silent reading performance. Judgments can then be made as to the efficiency of this performance in relation to national silent reading norms and attainable goals. In essence, eye-movement recording evaluates "how" a reader reads. While reading rate is one measure of fluency in silent reading, what comprises the process of silent reading can be accessed only through eye-movement recording. It is important to realize that for almost 200 years, beginning with Muller (1826) and Javal (1879), eye-movement behavior in reading has been evaluated by hundreds of researchers to make judgments as to a reader's efficiency and fluency in silent reading. There are over 100 such eye-movement references cited by Carmichael and Dearborn (1947), E. A. Taylor (1937), and Yarbus (1967) in relation to silent reading and to date no eye-movement studies have been published with regard to oral reading and its effect on silent reading.

READ-ALONG EXPERIENCES

Because there is a close relationship between oral reading and read-along (reading while listening) techniques, this latter practice should also be considered. It has long been demonstrated by Carbo (1978), Chomsky (1972), Heckelman (1969), and Van der Leif (1981) that read-along experiences are beneficial for many students. This is especially true when the rate of narration is very close to a student's usual silent reading rate. If narration rates, however, are too slow, excess fixations and regressions will emerge, as will be the case with listening to any oral reading that is slower than an individual's silent reading rate. On the other hand, if the rate is too fast, students will be inclined to depart from reading and simply start listening. For these reasons, S. E. Taylor (1965), in a "Bimodal Reading Methods Patent," stated that a variable playback rate must be used during read-along practice to allow students to select their own "best" playback rate to achieve proper audio reinforcement for visual input during reading. Biemiller, Bowden, Mackinnon, and Weinberg (1976) indicated that the speed (in words per minute) of a taped narration should be no faster than the child could read the same material orally. In the study by Shany and Biemiller (1995), tape speeds were varied between 80 to 120 wpm, and "each child selected the rate which was most agreeable to him or her." Reitsma (1988) commented that poorer readers profited less than better readers from read-along practice because presentation rates were too high for the less gifted readers." Carbo (1978) and Neville (1975) found that slowing narration rate could be beneficial but that slowing it too much seemed to result in comprehension problems. McMahon

(1956) commented that, "If the rate is too slow, the children may become bored and lose interest in the story and activity." Bergman (1999) stated, "Talking books should be narrated at a rate that matches or slightly exceeds the listener's silent reading rate."

If a proper rate balance is maintained between a narration and a student's silent reading, bimodal reinforcement will be achieved, which will allow either aural context preparation for word(s) to be encountered (pronunciation just ahead of fixation on a word) or a beneficial "rehearsal" process (hearing the word just previously fixated on). When there is only a slight difference (perhaps one word) between a student's silent reading of content and then hearing it, word recognition will be reinforced and the listening experience will then lead to an appreciation of proper expression of syntax and punctuation by the fluent expressive narration.

Thus, narration rates (hopefully adjustable) must be carefully considered in the future with regard to read-along approaches to reading development.

CONCLUSION

There is no doubt that oral reading can assist silent reading when there is a balance of practice in both oral and silent reading. Since efficiency in silent reading is a prime concern because of its effect on rate and comprehension, it is essential for educators to understand the effects of oral reading on silent reading.

FLUENCY IN SILENT READING

We live in a silent reading world. Students leave oral reading behind for the most part by the intermediate grades. From that point forward, they use silent reading in most learning and life situations. Further, silent reading is assessed in most standardized and state tests, but there is no widely accepted definition of proficiency in silent reading or widespread awareness of the most effective techniques for developing fluency in silent reading. It is also essential to better understand the nature of silent reading in terms of the skills that are essential to developing silent reading fluency and the training techniques that can be used to improve these skills.

The section that follows is a brief elaboration on the nature of each of the key skills or components of fluency in silent reading. It is acknowledged that many of these skills impinge on and interact with one another, and so references will be made among them at times.

In addition, numerous references will necessarily also be made to computerized fluency development programs, such as those provided in the Reading Plus® system, which have been specifically and uniquely designed to improve the visual, perceptual, and information processing skills that are essential to fluency in silent reading.

SKILLS OF SILENT READING FLUENCY

To better understand the nature of fluency in silent reading and the skills that must be adequately developed for meaningful levels of fluency to emerge, consider the following areas of proficiency:

1. Adequate near-point vision
2. Attention and concentration
3. Visual/functional proficiency (binocular coordination and vergence, oculomotility, and accuracy in tracking)
4. Perceptual accuracy/word recognition automaticity (accuracy in perceiving letters and letter order, instant word recognition, and visual memory)
5. Information processing efficiency (rapid and sequential input of word impressions into short-term memory)
6. Reading vocabulary
7. Comprehension capability
8. Adequate silent reading rates
9. Language and experiential background

Items two through five comprise what is termed by S. E. Taylor as the "Fundamental Reading Process." This process can be developed directly and effectively only through the use of a systematic silent fluency development course of study. The visual/functional, perceptual, and information processing skills that allow fluency in silent reading to emerge can be improved expediently only through the use of computer technology software. A teacher cannot direct this subliminal silent reading process (which functions three to five times per second as students move their eyes across lines of print in reading). Nor can students control their reading process, nor should they try to do so. Only through the visual/functional and perceptual modeling adjustments students make while engaged in computerized silent reading fluency training, will they alter the visual and perceptual processes that influence their efficiency in silent reading and resulting comprehension.

Adequate Vision

Beyond tests for adequacy of distance vision (typically what is evaluated today, at best), near-point vision must also be screened. Many students who can see well at a distance (20–20 at 20 feet) still see words as a blur, or in a less distinct fashion than desirable at usual reading distances (16–21 inches). Then too there are the learning and studying tasks of looking back and forth from the blackboard or whiteboard to the page that require good accommodation (quick change of focus). Finally, there is the student's ability to use both eyes as a team without suppression of vision in one eye or the other. Good vision is an essential first requirement in reading and learning, and certainly a key consideration when assessing the development of fluency in reading. There are screening techniques such as Bernell's N.Y.S.O.A. (Screening Kit 2002) that can be used to evaluate a student's near-point competence. Certainly students exhibiting difficulty in learning to read should be assessed in terms of near-point vision. Such screenings are essential if other factors of reading and learning are to take place adequately.

The College of Optometrists in Vision Development (COVD) stated logically that, "Vision is a contributing factor to an individual's ability to attend and respond to classroom instruction." The American Optometric Association (AOA) stated that, "Approximately one-half of those three years of age or older require treatment for a vision problem." The National Parent-Teacher Association (PTA) adopted a resolution (1999) calling for more adequate visual screening procedures. Now, it is also recommended by COVD that students be given an eye-movement recording appraisal, such as that provided for by the Visagraph® eye-movement recording system, to screen for visual/functional impediments.

Attention and Concentration

To better understand human cognition and comprehension, a consideration of attention, memory, and what is termed the "executive function," as cited by Lyons and Krasnegor (1999) is critical.

Attention is the ability to focus the mind on a single activity or concept. It can be consciously, voluntarily directed or involuntarily attracted. Mirsky (1999) defined it by saying, "We consider that attention represents a highly articulated form of consciousness that has been shaped and modified by leaning and experience."

A first consideration is a student's ability to focus attention on the task of reading, direct the eyes toward print, and become actively involved in the reading task and understanding. Many children lack this very basic ability to focus and direct their attention in learning activities. These children must be given practice activities that require a strong focus on building attention. Attention can be trained through computer software that provides scanning and flashing activities with letters, words, and text.

One of the biggest challenges facing teachers at every level is to find ways to help students focus and maintain attention on a given task. Reading is one of the primary tasks for which maintaining attention is essential. According to Torgesen and Hudson (2006):

> A fluent reader can maintain this performance for long periods of time, retain the skill after long periods of no practice, and can generalize across texts. A fluent reader is also not easily distracted and reads in an effortless, flowing manner.

This would suggest that one of the defining characteristics of a proficient silent reader is the ability to sustain attention. The question then arises: Can attention be trained? McIlvane, Dube, and Callahan (1999) asserted that:

> . . . general improvements in attending may be attainable through the right kind of training. When attention is viewed as a fixed resource, the Improvement route is to teach the individual to allocate that resource more efficiently; that is, to improve executive functioning. Behavior analysts tend to assume that attending itself can be made more efficient–that the attentional resources can be expanded.

Next, there is the aspect of concentration or the ability to sustain attention. James (1890) referred to concentration as being "dependent upon repeated redirection of effort to the focus of attention and resistance to attractions that co-exist in the process." Again, it is essential to first consider a student's visual adjustment to the near-point activity of reading. Attention and concentration will naturally be greatly influenced by a student's vision and visual ease and comfort in reading. Studies by Carmichael and Dearborn (1947) documented that students should be able to read in a sustained manner for up to two hours without visual fatigue. However, any extraordinary energy consumed to maintain binocular coordination (resulting in clear and single vision), expended in head movement (as opposed to the rotation of the eyes), or inefficient oculomotor efforts to stay on lines of print can cause discomfit that will lead to "breaks" in concentration. Research reports by Schlange (1999) and Johnson, Nottingham, Stratton, and Zaba (1996) suggested that attentional difficulties with ADD and ADHD students may, in part, stem from visual/functional inadequacies. Getz (1980) stated, "Where vision is difficult and requires greater effort than normal, the child will usually exhibit an avoidance reaction to near-point work, and thus appear not to be trying or 'day-dreaming.' "Also, if the process of reading overall is too slow and laborious, which is the case with many beginning readers who typically read at rates far below their usual listening and speaking rates, there is the tendency for "minds to wander."

These periodic lapses in attention will be more prevalent among poor readers. Lapses in focus of attention and concentration will result in the tendency to reread frequently to maintain comprehension. While rereading in study type activities is certainly acceptable at times to reflect, visualize, and analyze, excessive or compulsive rereading is not acceptable.

The ability to concentrate is very dependent on visual ease, perceptual efficiency, and the rate and efficiency with which information is processed. A study by Solan (2001) showed that attention increased as students developed greater reading proficiency using the engaging activities provided by computer-delivered programs including scanning and flashing activities.

Another consideration of memory in relation to attention and concentration relates to the ability of a student to continue to read if continuous understanding and recollection of what has been read is not achieved. It is evident that inefficient processing of visual information and its translation into memory will greatly affect a student's comprehension and ultimately his or her ability and desire to continue to attend to the reading task. Considerations of necessary information processing capabilities and comprehension skills are treated in later sections.

A fourth consideration, cited by Pennington, Bennetto, McNeer, and Roberts (1999), is termed the executive function, which would seem to relate to a student's ability to direct attention in relation to specific cognitive needs and apply strategies to achieve certain goals of understanding. In reading, there is a dual need to maintain attention and concentration as an ongoing function to achieve literal comprehension, the flexibility to direct the mind to the ideas and suggestions being expressed by the author, and to relate information to personal experiences and needs. This executive function of attention may signal the need to reread for clarification of what has been read, to pause and think about what had been suggested but not stated, or simply to reflect and organize. In essence, the executive function exerts more influence as higher-level cognitive skills of analysis, evaluation, and appreciation are required or applied.

In summary, a student needs to possess the ability to concentrate for meaningful fluency in silent reading to emerge, and good literal comprehension to be attained, in preparation for employing higher-level cognitive skills.

Visual/Functional Proficiency

It is important to understand that the near-point activity of reading is not a natural human act. However, we must accomplish necessary visual adjustments in order to become fluent readers. As stated previously, The National PTA's (1999) resolution related to "Learning Related Vision Problems" stated, "Knowledge regarding the relationship between poorly developed visual skills and poor academic performance is not widely held among students, parents, teachers, administrators and public health officials." The PTA resolution recommended more adequate visual screening of both vision and visual/functional proficiency.

It is essential to efficient fluent silent reading that a student maintain both good binocular coordination and vergence (team use of both eyes), possess acceptable oculomotility (the ability to rotate the eyes and not the head), and track accurately (staying on the line and progressing sequentially across lines of print with good left to right directional attack).

If a student does not have good visual/functional skills, reading will not be a comfortable activity, and this can result in poor attention and concentration. Further, poor visual skills can cause a student to see print in a blurred or muddy fashion, interfering with accuracy of word recognition. Stated simply, if the student cannot function well visually, it is unlikely that fluency in silent reading will occur.

Studies by Atzmon (1993), Getz (1980), Heath, Cook, and O'Dell (1976), Punnett and Steinhauer (1984), and Steinman and Steinman (1999), in which only visual/functional training was administered, showed distinct improvement in reading even though remedial reading instruction was not provided. In studies by Seiderman (1980), Solan (2001), Streff, Poynter, Jinks, and Wolff (1990), and Waldstricker (1962), in which visual training was combined with reading instruction, substantial gains in reading were achieved by the students involved.

Further, in-school visual training programs such as those administered by Hellerstein, Danner, Maples, Press, Schneebeck, and Miller (2001) and Hoover and Harris (1997) also documented the value of visual training combined with computerized reading fluency development training and both involved the use of the Visagraph® eye-movement recording system in pre- and post-testing. Finally, in an eye-movement study by Schlange (1999), in which computerized fluency training that provided timed and directed left to right presentations of print without the support of visual/functional training did also develop higher levels of visual/functional efficiency as revealed by pre- and post-measurements of eye movement.

In summary, it is critical that visual/functional efficiency be developed for meaningful levels of fluency in silent reading to emerge and for ease and comfort in reading to be experienced.

Perceptual Accuracy/Word Recognition Automaticity

A student's ability to accurately discriminate letters, realize letter order, and recognize words instantly is a basic requirement for fluency in silent reading to emerge. Students need to be able to instantly and accurately recognize the orthographic structure of words, which they will subsequently identify as a given word and then proceed to word association.

A reader's eyes will typically move three to five times per second as the previously cited study by S. E. Taylor and Robinson (1963) showed. Beginning readers arrive at school with observational habits that prompt them to keep their eyes in motion three times a second. If words cannot be instantly recognized in one-third of a second or less, a beginning reader will resort to multiple fixations (eye-stops) to perceive words. Over time, the tendency to make multiple fixations and regressions (more eye-movements) will become part of a student's conditioned oculomotor activity, which will become relatively habitual as a student progresses to the intermediate grades. These multiple fixations and regressions, and the wandering visual approach to reading, will ultimately inhibit a reader's ease and comfort in reading, limit reading rate, as well as reduce comprehension.

According to Pikulski (2006):

> This instant, accurate, and automatic access to all these dimensions of a printed word is the needed fluency that will allow readers to focus their attention on comprehension rather than on decoding. According to Ehri (1995, 1998), careful processing of print in the fully alphabetic stage leads to this rapid, instant recognition. Partial alphabetic readers store incomplete representations of words and, therefore, confuse similar words such as were, where, wire, and wore. However, once the word form is fully processed, with repeated encounters of the word, it is recognized instantly and accurately.
>
> . . . Readers who have reached this stage also develop another valuable, attention-saving, effective decoding skill. In addition to storing words as units, repeated encounters with words allow a reader to store letter patterns across different words.

Torgesen and Hudson (2006) reported that:

> . . . many students with reading disabilities may have special difficulties acquiring fully developed orthographic representations, even after they

become accurate readers. Although the precise nature of the underlying difficulty associated with this problem is not clear at this point, the problem itself would mean that these students would require even more accurate practice trials than normal readers to create reliable orthographic representations.

Whether word recognition is approached from a sight word or a phonetic standpoint, it is essential that the letter order configuration be accurately and instantly perceived. Fortunately, this basic skill of "seeing the word correctly" is quite trainable with today's computer software that provides scanning and flashing practice with letters and words. Not only does developing orthographic accuracy aid the development of instant word recognition, but it also facilitates improved spelling abilities, which are also dependent on visual memory.

La Berge and Samuels (1973) and Logan (1997) cited the need for automaticity in word recognition in order that time and attention be devoted during each eye-pause to the realization of syntax and understanding of what is read. In essence, if word recognition is overly time-consuming, and especially if multiple fixations are required to recognize words, there is little time and attention left to devote to the meaning of what is being read. It is essential that word recognition in silent reading must be accomplished in only a fraction of the length of a typical eye-pause time (perhaps only .10 sec. out of the usual eye-pause time of .33 sec. for beginning readers) for attention to be devoted to realizing syntax and to achieving good understanding. The National Reading Panel (2000) further reinforced this need in their report, which states, "Skilled readers also get better at seeing a word in a single fixation; therefore evidence fewer refixations on the same words and fewer regressions in which they have to look back at a word again after they have read other words." The supporting studies referred to in the report are Frazier and Rayner (1982), Kennedy and Murray (1988), Kennedy and Murray (1978, 1987a, 1987b), McConkie and Zola (1979), and Rayner, McConkie, and Zola (1980).

Further, a study by Gilbert (1959), cited previously, indicated that multiple fixations to recognize words are especially detrimental in reading for poorer readers. The shifting to different viewing points (multiple directions) to recognize words was perceptually confusing to poorer readers.

Consider that in a typical Grade 1 beginning reading program, a large number of new words are typically introduced in basal reading or reading anthology approaches each week without "flash" training to make these words instantly recognizable (automatic). Delayed or slow word recognition will naturally encourage the need for multiple fixations and eventually condition a random oculomotor activity. Then, too slow or less efficient oral reading as cited previously, can encourage multiple fixations and random visual wandering during reading. Finally, any tendency to "overdecode" or to direct too much conscious attention to the decoding process during silent reading can result in multiple fixations per word that will eventually become habitual.

It is acknowledged that extensive reading and encouraging students to read more are approaches to improving word recognition. However, most poor readers will not typically read extensively, for they are not efficient and do not enjoy reading. Stanovich (1980) cited the Matthew effect in reading, taken from the Bible chapter on Matthew, "The rich get richer and the poor get poorer." He stated poor readers read less than good readers and so, after time, the gap increases between poor readers and those who are more accomplished.

Over the years it has been demonstrated again and again that "flash" (tachistoscopic) techniques, or rapid and timed left-to-right reading content exposures can be used effectively and directly to develop instant word recognition of all reading vocabulary. It should be clarified that flash training, in which words are exposed for such brief intervals as one sixth of a second or shorter, does not allow time for a student to move his or her eyes. Thus, as stated previously, the flashed material must be retained from a single "glimpse" or fixation. With such single impression training, students can acquire proficiency in letter identification and realization of letter order (orthographic competence), as well as a stronger visual memory.

Aiken (1896), Cattell (1885), and Volkmann (1859), and later Davis (1956), Rusk (1915), Weber (1937), and Wilkins (1917) all documented the value of tachistoscopic or "flash" practice on word recognition, reading, and learning. Today's computer software that provides rapid recognition of letters and letter order can develop high levels of visual discrimination and build a strong visual memory. Beyond this, flash training techniques can make the recognition of core or high-frequency reading vocabulary considerably more instant. Finally, there is computer software today that continues to develop rapid word recognition as a continuous reading process, while simultaneously encouraging a more sequential left-to-right visual intake process, all of which allows more rapid and successful association of words ("chunking" of words to realize larger syntactical units), which in turn leads to a more complete realization of what is read.

Early eye-movement studies by E. A. Taylor (1937) and Witzeman (1941), and, more recently, the use of the Visagraph® eye-movement recording technique, documented the dramatic changes that can be made in silent reading by training visual/functional proficiency, word recognition automaticity, and improved information processing. Changes in these basic skills result in more rapid and accurate information processing, which produces improved comprehension and eventually leads to significant improvement in standardized test performance, as cited by Rasinski, Samuels, Hiebert, Petscher, and Feller (2011) in a study in Miami, Florida, involving 16,143 students in grades 4 and 10.

Additional studies over the years by Arundel (1957); Beckly (1963); Bottomly (1961); Brickner and Senter (1969); Gelzer and Santore (1968); Hetrick and Wilson (1968); Hoffman (1966); Malone (1964); McDowell (1969); Ruck (1982); Solan (1987); Solan (2001); Solan, Feldman, and Tajak (1995); and Thompson (1956) have all shown conclusively that Controlled Reading, Guided Reading and/or tachistoscopic training (flash training) can lead to improved oculomotor behavior and improved comprehension. Interestingly, the judgment that reading research had produced sufficient documentation to support the use of reading technology to improve reading was stated years ago by Traxler (1935). In the last 50 years, and especially in the last 10 years, there have been many more research reports or studies by schools and universities citing the gains made through the use of reading fluency development technology as measured by the Visagraph® eye-movement recording system and standardized reading tests.

A reader's efficiency in silent reading can be studied through eye-movement recordings, which measure the average number of fixations (eye stops) per word, and the average length of time of these fixations. According to S. E. Taylor et al. (1960), in the primary grades, students will require, on average, 2.24 fixations (or eye stops) in grade 1 and up to 1.55 fixations in grade 3 to process, or recognize, each word. The average time to recognize each word ranges from .73 seconds to .43 seconds. Samuels (2006) reinforced this when he said that, ". . . research using a variety of techniques consistently found that the size of the visual unit used in word recognition by beginning readers is smaller than the entire word." These "visual units" refer to what is taken in with each fixation. In the intermediate grades through high school, students make close to a single fixation per word with the fixation lasting from .27 seconds to .24 seconds. As stated previously, for truly fluent reading, a student needs to spend less time and attention to recognize words, leaving the majority of fixation time for attention to word association and comprehension.

Information Processing Efficiency

It is evident from all research to date that word recognition automaticity (instant word recognition) and an improved directional attack will permit more rapid and sequential realization of syntax. Smith (1973) stated, "Reading comprehension is reduced below listening comprehension when reading is slow, causing overload to short-term memory."

In usual silent reading, visual impressions are fed to the mind (short-term memory) 3 to 5 times per second. The ability of short-term memory to maintain and interpret the information is influenced by levels of attention and concentration, reading rate (time to receive visual information and store this in short-term memory) and the sequence of impressions (influenced by the nature of directional attack), which results in orderliness, or lack of it, in the word intake process. This input process influences a student's ability to "chunk" information, decreasing the number of units to be held in short-term memory as cited by Miller (1956). Thus, the information processing capability of a student is highly dependent on the accuracy, speed, and orderliness of the visual input process. Many have referred to computerized fluency development techniques that employ timed left-to-right displays of text as eye-movement training. While this is undoubtedly true to some extent, the ultimate value of fluency training lies in developing a more orderly visual input process (directional attack), instant recognition of words (automaticity), and the encouragement of more rapid associational processes, all of which lead to improved reading rate and comprehension, as well as greater ease and comfort and sustained attention in reading.

As mentioned previously, some have referred to the left-to-right presentation of print as providing a "modeling" visual/perceptual intake experience for beginning readers. One child reported, "It's just like someone speaking to you."

Oral reading in the early grades can certainly contribute to a student's awareness of phrasing, but in silent reading in later grades, a student needs to realize phrases far more rapidly. The configuration of words perceived and word association, in terms of the meaning expressed by a phrase, lags behind the visual intake of words. Wagner (1999) reinforced this concept, "Presumably the contents of short-term memory would lag behind the eyes with a three- to four-word delay corresponding to the eye-voice span" (p. 144).

To promote the realization of phrases in silent reading, a student needs to read swiftly through the words of each sentence, "risk taking" at intervals in terms of word identification, and later confirming both the words perceived and the realization of phrases in relation to meaning. Many times the meaning of certain words will change as a student completes the reading of a particular sentence or sentences. Words will vary to the extent that they will be instantly identified and recognized later. Context prior to and following the perception of a word undoubtedly reinforces word recognition and encourages phrasing.

Reading Vocabulary

When considering a reading vocabulary, there are two aspects to be considered: instant sight vocabulary and word meaning and use. It is evident that students need to amass a larger instant sight vocabulary if they are to achieve fluency in silent reading. Torgesen and Hudson (2006) cited an older study when they said:

> In an earlier analysis (Torgesen, Rashotte, & Alexander, 2001), we provided substantial evidence that the single most important factor in accounting for individual differences in reading fluency among students with reading disabilities was the speed with which individual words are recognized.

Today's software that provides flash (tachistoscopic) training as well as timed, left-to-right displays of continuous text can help students enlarge their instant silent reading vocabulary.

Torgesen and Hudson (2006) later said, "This limitation of 'sight word' vocabulary is a principal characteristic of most children with reading disabilities after the initial phase in learning to read." They proposed a solution when they said:

> . . . effective interventions for students struggling with reading fluency must substantially increase the number of opportunities these students have to accurately practice reading previously unknown words. Both techniques that provide reading practice in connected text (Hudson, Lane, & Pullen, 2005; Meyer & Felton, 1999) and those that provide practice in reading words in isolation (Levy, 2001; Levy, Abello, & Lysnchuk, 1997; Tan & Nicholson, 1997) have been shown to improve reading fluency and proficiency in struggling readers.

What words to address becomes the next question. Hiebert (2006) reported:

> It has long been recognized that a relatively small number of words account for a substantial percentage of total words encountered in reading (Thorndike, 1921). Based on a sample of 17.25 million words in texts used from kindergarten through college, Zeno, Ivens, Millard, and Duvvuri (1995) reported that 25 words account for 33% of the total words in the corpus. When the number of different words gets to around 5,575, approximately 90% of the total words in texts from third through ninth grade (Carol et al., 1971) and about 80% of the total words in texts from kindergarten through college (Zeno et al., 1995) are accounted for.

Pressley, Gaskins, and Fingeret (2006) cited the work of Dolch and his creation of the 1,000 most commonly encountered words as highly significant and further stated, "Dolch's idea of making certain that students know a core set of commonly encountered words makes even more sense today in light of some recent analyses." They went on to say:

> The best texts for aiding struggling readers to become fluent readers appear to be those that have a controlled vocabulary consisting of a high percentage of both high-frequency words (e.g., the, dog) and words with consistent and decodable patterns (e.g., rug, sun).

Hiebert (2006) further reinforced the need for students to encounter a high-frequency vocabulary with frequent repetitions while working with struggling readers:

> A question that educators frequently ask is whether texts that consist almost of highly frequent and phonetically regular words also can be engaging and merit rereading for different purposes. In a previous era, controlled texts were common in schools.
> In some locations, teachers may find that the storerooms of county and district offices have old textbook programs. As the re-analysis of the NRP fluency study showed (Hiebert & Fisher, 2005), textbooks prior to the late 1980s and early 1990s exaggerate high-frequency words.

There appears to be a general agreement that repeated exposures to high-frequency vocabulary and procedures to accomplish more rapid word recognition are essential to establishing a sight word reading vocabulary with beginning readers as well as with more advanced readers. Today's software provides such extensive high-frequency vocabulary encounters in a wide variety of reading genres.

There also seems to be widespread agreement that extensive reading facilitated by more fluent reading is one of the best means of expanding a student's reading vocabulary.

Beyond extensive reading, there are other approaches to expanding or enriching reading vocabulary. Among these is the use of structured cloze practice to develop analytical reading and context clues strategies. Cloze has been defined as any procedure that omits portions of text and asks readers to resupply the missing elements (Oller & Jonz, 1994). It is a measure of reading comprehension that is based on the psychology that humans have a tendency to complete patterns. These typically emphasize the following context clue strategies in nontimed meaning completion and vocabulary-building cloze activities:

1. Same Meaning/Synonyms
2. Opposite Meaning/Antonym
3. Association/Synthesis
4. Categorization/Classification
5. Time/Order
6. Signal Words, Phrases/Transitions
7. Pronoun Referents
8. Similarities/Differences
9. Form/Function
10. Conclusion/Summary
11. Definition

Computer-delivered modified cloze techniques, wherein selected words are deleted, encourage a student to use and learn to employ the context skills listed previously to complete meaning and to further appreciate the use of particular words. Vocabulary development activities that employ contextual analysis activities as a means of encouraging students to use the context surrounding words to fully appreciate the meaning and use of vocabulary contained in graded reading selections are especially helpful in developing comprehension competence. As stated by Greenwood and Flanigan (2007):

> Because they are so transportable, context clues merit careful teaching. Students need to be sensitized to the various types of context clues that are available to them–they need to gradually become aware that authors choose their words carefully.

Learning to become sensitive to contextual clues can be truly mastered only through intensive practice. While a teacher might describe a particular contextual analysis strategy, its use repeatedly during actual reading practice is essential for true mastery.

Comprehension Capability

Comprehension competence is first determined by a student's ease and comfort in reading, which influences his or her level of attention and ability to concentrate. Next, the visual input process must be truly efficient for short-term memory to function efficiently to result in information processing effectiveness and understanding. Beyond this, there are the considerations of the specific cognitive processes and comprehension skills.

There are several accepted approaches to comprehension development. Among these are extensive practice reading activities combined with thorough comprehension questioning, providing single comprehension skill lessons that explain and ask the student to apply particular cognitive skill, KWL (exercises where students record "what I know, what I want to know, and what I have learned"), and teacher-guided discussions directing student attention to vocabulary and concepts that will lead to better understanding. Other methods of teaching comprehension have been the subject of recent scrutiny and research. One such major area of research and discussion is the use of repeated reading as cited previously.

Samuels (2006) cited the Report of the National Reading Panel (2000) and his own research in support of repeated reading's effect on reading fluency. It is expected that, in some cases, repeated readings, as perceived by Samuels, can assist in comprehension development.

However, in addition to, or in conjunction with repeated reading, students need to read extensively. Allington (2006a) observed:

> . . . Kuhn (2005a, 2005b) found that extensive independent-reading activity produced comprehension gains that the repeat reading did not. She notes that . . . a focus on simply reading fluently in repeated-reading interventions may bias students in a manner that undermines developing an intention to understand what is being read.

It is also important to consider what reading content to use in reading development approaches that would elevate both reading fluency and comprehension. Allington (2006b) concluded:

> . . . students who exhibit dysfluent reading . . . are too often children whose dysfluency is but a signal that they have been routinely given the wrong texts, texts that are too difficult. They often then avoid trying to read these texts, but when they do read, they struggle . . .
> The intervention I would propose is straightforward. Provide these children with high-success reading experiences all day long. Fill their desks with books they can read accurately, fluently, and with understanding.

Topping (2006) reinforced this when he said, "Fluency is not likely to be developed on material that is much too hard or easy." This emphasizes that it is imperative for reading content difficulty to be matched to students' current fluency levels if students are to further develop their fluency and comprehension skills.

The work of O'Connor and colleagues (2002) as reported by Allington (2006b) showed that:

> . . . providing daily intervention lessons using grade-level texts was not nearly as successful as providing daily lessons using texts matched to the reading level of struggling readers. Given that selecting texts that are of appro-

priate complexity for learners is the first step in the design of effective instruction. O'Connor and colleagues wonder why anyone would think that matching intervention texts to readers would not also be the first step in planning effective intervention.

Assuming then, that the practice reading content is appropriate for each student, comprehension building activities must be provided that enable a student to develop comprehension competence.

There are two fundamental means of developing more effective cognitive processing. One is that of inductive practice (learning by doing), in which a more global comprehension approach is employed during reading. If a broad array of cognitive skill questions is posed in conjunction with each new reading experience, a student will soon learn to read in a global and comprehensive manner and will grow in overall comprehension competency. This age-old "practice reading" approach has been used for years effectively. In this regard, research by Stanovich (1980) strongly suggested that a truly fluent reader should read with complete "openness" to what will be encountered without trying to anticipate the nature and the direction of the printed message. Anticipation of information, and then different information actually experienced, can cause reorganization or rejection, which can cause a student to realign his or her thinking. This is nonproductive time and counterproductive in terms of good comprehension.

A second approach to building comprehension competence is to provide single skill instruction in particular cognitive processes (i.e., specific lessons in drawing conclusions, comparing and contrasting, categorizing, etc.). As a student recognizes what is required in these specific cognitive processes, he or she will store away this awareness for later use in global inductive reading experiences. Remediation of specific skills has also been employed for years. However, when considering this remedial approach to comprehension development, it should be noted that many skills relate to other skills and are not totally exclusive in nature. Further, single skill comprehension lessons will typically be written to clearly demonstrate the nature of a particular cognitive process and, as a result, will not be presented as clearly in the context of usual reading. For this reason, single skill remediation is limited, and best employed as a supplement to global inductive reading approaches.

In computerized fluency development programs such as the Guided Reading program,[1] there is strong emphasis on developing a wide diversity

---

1. In this chapter, the term guided reading will be used. This term has evolved from the use of the Guided Read™, a device used in the 1980s to develop fluency in silent reading. Today, many educators also use the term "guided reading" to describe teacher-directed small-group reading enhancement activities. In this chapter and subsequent chapters, the term "guided reading" will be used to describe timed left-to-right displays of text to develop fluency in silent reading.

of comprehension skills through extensive reading as students read appropriate-level selections and answer accompanying comprehension questions. These skills in the following list are treated again and again in global inductive reading exercises.

1. Literal Understanding
   1-1 Recalling Information and Details
   1-2 Following Sequence of Ideas or Events
   1-3 Identifying Speaker
2. Interpretation
   2-1 Determining Main Idea
   2-2 Making Inferences
   2-3 Predicting Outcomes
   2-4 Drawing Conclusions
   2-5 Interpreting Figurative Language
   2-6 Visualizing
   2-7 Paraphrasing
3. Analysis
   3-1 Comparing and Contrasting
   3-2 Recognizing Cause and Effect
   3-3 Classifying
   3-4 Reasoning
   3-5 Identifying Analogies
4. Evaluation
   4-1 Detecting Author's Purpose
   4-2 Understanding Persuasion
   4-3 Recognizing Slant and Bias
   4-4 Distinguishing Between Fact and Opinion
   4-5 Judging Validity
   4-6 Determining Relative Importance
5. Appreciation
   5-1 Interpreting Character
   5-2 Recognizing Emotional Reactions
   5-3 Identifying Mood and Tone
   5-4 Identifying Setting

In addition, supplemental "away from the computer" single skill lessons in many of the above listed skills can be provided as needed. During these skill lessons explanations and applications of a specific cognitive process are explored and then practiced. Teacher intervention, in small groups, offering guidance about these skill explanations can provide direction as to the thought processes that can be employed in usual reading.

Language Experiences and Experiential Background

Language experience, developed adequately prior to reading, undoubtedly influences a reader's ability to realize information during reading. It is essential that teachers, especially when complying to the needs of ESL and other students with limited oral language background, adequately prepare students in both language and concepts for the reading experiences to follow. These activities are best provided through teacher-guided oral language development activities. Then, when students become involved with guided reading lessons, they will capitalize on this expanded language experience as a basis for better understanding in reading.

It is undoubtedly true that experiential background, in general, is a key determinant of the student's ability to understand and apply what is read. It then follows that extensive reading experiences can provide a wealth of language experience development. However, extensive reading will occur only if the student is truly an accomplished fluent silent reader and finds "real freedom to read and learn."

Adequate Silent Reading Rates

According to Rasinski and Lenhart (2007), "Reading rate (how fast one reads) seems to have emerged as the key defining characteristic of reading fluency, and so fluency has come to be assessed through measurements of reading rate." Obviously, rate and comprehension have to function together. Rate without good comprehension is meaningless. Thus, fluency in reading means adequate reading rate with good comprehension as well as ease and comfort in reading that facilitates attention.

When addressing the need for fluency in silent reading there are many references today to automaticity of word recognition (instant word recognition) and rates of reading. So it is essential to look first at the national normative silent reading rates children exhibit at various grade levels and also at reasonable and achievable silent reading rate goals for each grade level. The Report of the National Reading Panel (2000) cited the norm reading performances developed by S. E. Taylor et al. (1960). Table 5.1, based on a study by S. E. Taylor, et al. (1960) study of over 12,000 students throughout the grades, shows normative rate performances as well as S. E. Taylor's projections as to reasonable silent reading rates at all levels. These rate goals have proven to be achievable by thousands of students who have used fluency development technology over the years.

For additional perspective, typical reading rates with nontrained students have been cited in studies by Buswell (1922), E. A. Taylor (1937), and Gilbert (1953) in Table 5.2.

Table 5.1

Taylor National Norms												
Grade Level	1	2	3	4	5	6	7	8	9	10	11	12
Norm Rates	80	115	138	158	173	185	195	204	214	224	237	250
Target Rates	140	170	200	230	250	270	280	300	310	325	345	365

Table 5.2

Grade Level	Grade 1 wpm	Grade 2 wpm	Grade 3 wpm	Grade 4 wpm	Grade 5 wpm	Grade 6 wpm
(10) Buswell (1922)	89	153	214	300	352	333
(91) Taylor, E. (1937)	55	90	115	168	190	200
(26) Gilbert (1953)	88	120	153	206	250	272

As an example of the need for higher rates than are typically achieved today, consider that beginning readers should logically achieve reading rates between 125 and 175 wpm, which would return their silent reading performances to their usual listening and speaking communication rates, as cited by Taylor (1964). Further, Taylor (1981) conducted a study of grade 1 and 2 students that reported reading rate achievements for grade 1 students of 136–146 wpm and grade 2 students achieving reading rates between 160 and 167 wpm. Further, a study by Shelley-Tremblay and Eyer (2009) with second graders reported silent reading rates around 150+ wpm after using fluency development software.

Beyond this, in the intermediate grades, it seems reasonable to expect silent reading rates to be above 200 wpm if students are to reduce the tendency to vocalize and to read more effectively and fluently in their content area studies.

At the secondary and college levels, the nature of assigned reading would seem to require that students accomplish reading rates of 300–400 wpm or higher to complete their studies in a reasonable period of time.

CONCLUSION

It would seem that appropriate measures of reading fluency or proficiency in silent reading should address all facets of the reading process, from vision through comprehension, and that new considerations must be given to evaluation of the most basic visual/functional, perceptual, and information processing skills not typically considered in most reading development programs. If students are to be able to read silently with good attention and concentration, ease and comfort, at adequate reading rates, and with good comprehension, these basic skills must be developed. It would seem likely that there will need to be a reconsideration of fluency development that would lead to a better balance between oral and silent reading practices to adequately capitalize on the benefits of both areas of development. Certainly, study of the effects of oral reading practice on the development of fluency in silent reading needs further exploration through eye-movement recording procedures. Lastly, it is apparent that development of the high-speed and largely subliminal processes of silent reading will best be provided through computerized training techniques to expeditiously provide the visual/perceptual and cognitive modeling process that will result in meaningful fluency in silent reading. How to provide for adequate use of computerized training techniques in the daily schedule of schools is a question to be solved and will be discussed in Chapter 6.

There is universal consensus today that we live in a silent reading world. Silent reading is constantly tested in most state and standardized reading tests. Most all reading, beyond the elementary grades, involves silent reading. Yet today, the majority of fluency research has focused largely on oral reading practices and evaluation. Likely, this has resulted from the fact that silent reading performance is difficult to evaluate beyond measures of reading rate. The high-speed (3–5 eye stops per second) silent reading process can be evaluated only through eye-movement recording. Fortunately, today, there are quick and easy eye-movement recording techniques (seven to eight minutes) that make it possible to evaluate "how" a student reads silently. Eye-movement research will undoubtedly lead to a better understanding of the more basic skills that comprise fluency, or efficiency, in silent reading. This information about the reading process when combined with standardized silent reading tests will provide a more complete evaluation and a true measure of a student's reading proficiency.

QUESTIONS THAT COULD ARISE
AFTER READING THIS CHAPTER

1. Why are visual/functional, perceptual, and information processing skills not evaluated today? Why are eye-movement recording techniques not employed?
2. What is the relationship between a lack of these basic skills and the needs of today's struggling readers? Can further improvement of these basic skills also help more advanced readers become more fluent readers?
3. What are the percentages of students who could benefit from fluency in silent reading development today? What would be the impact on the learning and vocational competence of these students?

REFERENCES

Aiken, C. (1896). *Methods of mind training.* New York: Harper and Brothers.

Allington, R. L. (2006a). Fluency: Still waiting after all these years. In S. J. Samuels & A. E. Farstrup (Eds.), *What research has to say about fluency instruction* (pp. 94–105). Newark, DE: International Reading Association.

Allington, R. L. (2006b). *What really matters for struggling readers: Designing research-based programs* (2nd ed.). Boston: Allyn & Bacon.

Arundel, Rev. E. (1957). Controlled reading at Sienna College. *Catholic Educator, 28,* 98–105.

Atzmon, D. (1993). A randomized masked comparative study of orthoptic treatment vs. conventional reading tutoring for reading disabilities. *Binocular Vision and Eye Muscle Surgery Quarterly, 8*(2), 91–106.

Beckly, L. L. (1963). The EDL Controlled Reader in an accelerated primary reading program. A Thesis for MS in Education Degree, Winona State College, Winona, Minnesota.

Bergman, O. (1999). *Wait for me! Reader control of narration rate in talking books.* Reading Online. The International Reading Association. Retrieved from http://www.readingonline.org /articles/bergman/wait.html

Bernell Corp. Deluxe School Screening Kit. (2002). www.bernell.com

Biemiller, A., Bowden, J., Mackinnon, L., & Weinberg, D. (1976). A pilot study of the procedure to increase reading speed at the fifth and sixth grade level. Unpublished paper. Institute of Child Study, University of Toronto.

Bottomly, F. (1961). An experiment with the Controlled Reader. *Journal of Educational Research, 54*(7), 265–269.

Brickner, A., & Senter, D. R. (1969). Reading practice attention by first year listen, look, learn students. *EDL Research and Information Report 2.* New York: EDL/McGraw-Hill.

Buswell, G. (1920). An experimental study of the eye-voice span in reading. *Supplemental Educational Monographs, No. 17,* University of Chicago Press, 1–105.

Buswell, G. (1922). Fundamental reading habits: A study of their development. *Supplementary Educational Monographs, No. 20,* University of Chicago Press, 150.

Carbo, M. (1978, December). Teaching reading with talking books. *The Reading Teacher,* 267–273.

Carmichael, L., & Dearborn, W. (1947). *Reading and visual fatigue.* Boston: Houghton Mifflin Company.

Cattell, J. (1885). The inertia of the eye and brain. *Brain, VIII,* 295–312.

Chomsky, C. (1972). Stages in language development and reading exposure. *Harvard Educational Review, 42,* 1–33.

Cook, D. L. (1956, Winter). Vision therapy and quality of life. *Journal of Optometric Vision Development, 26*(18).

Davis, L. F. (1956). The S.V.E. Speed-i-o-Scope, an investment for school learning. *Visual Review, 50*(1), *Society for Visual Education, 1*(7). *Journal of Educational Psychology, 94*(3), 474–485.

Edformation, Inc. (2000–2001 School Year). Oral reading fluency normative performance chart. Eden Prairie, MN: Edformation, Inc.

Feinberg, R. (1949). A study of some aspects of peripheral visual acuity. *Archives of American Academy of Optometrics, 26,* 49–56 and 105–119.

Frazier, L., & Rayner, K. (1982). Making and correcting errors during sentence comprehension: Eye movements in the analysis of structurally ambiguous sentences. *Cognitive Psychology, 14,* 178–210.

Gelzer, A., & Santore, N. J. (1968). A comparison of various reading input approaches. *Journal of Educational Research, 61*(6), 267–272.

Getz, D. J. (1980). Learning enhancement through visual training. *Academic Therapy, 15*(4), 457–466.

Gilbert, L. C. (1940, April). Effect on silent reading of attempting to follow oral reading. *Elementary School Journal, 40,* 614–621.

Gilbert, L. C. (1953). Functional motor efficiency of the eyes and its relation to reading. *University of California Publications in Education, II*(3), 159–231. Berkeley: University of California Press.

Gilbert, L. C. (1959, February). Saccadic movements as a factor in visual perception in reading. *Journal of Educational Psychology, 50,* 15–19.

Glass, G. (1973). *Teaching decoding as separate from reading.* New York: Adelphi University.

Greenwood, S. C., & Flanigan, K. (2007). Overlapping vocabulary and comprehension context and clues compliments semantic gradients. *The Reading Teacher, 61*(3), 249–254.

Hasbrouck, J. E., & Tindal, G. (1992). Curriculum basal oral reading fluency norms for students in grades 2–5. *Teacher of Exceptional Children, 24*(3), 41–44.

Hasbrouck, J., & Tindal, G. A. (2006). Oral reading fluency norms: A valuable assessment tool for reading teachers. *The Reading Teacher, 59,* 636–644.

Heath, E. J., Cook, P., & O'Dell, N. (1976). Eye exercises and reading efficiency. *Academic Therapy, XI*(4), 435–445.

Hebb, D. O. (1949). *The organization of behavior: A neuropsychological theory.* New York: John Wiley & Sons, Inc.

Heckelman, R. G. (1969). A neurological impress method of reading instruction. *Academic Therapy, 44,* 278–282.

Hellerstein, L. F., Danner, R., Maples, W. C., Press, L., Schneebeck, J., & Miller, S. (2001, Summer). Optometric guidelines for school consulting. *Journal of Optometric Vision Development, 32*(2), 56–75.

Hendricks, A. W., & Kolk, H. H. J. (1997). Strategic control in developmental dyslexia. *Cognitive Neuropsychology, 14,* 321–366.

Hetrick, W. M., & Wilson, F. R. (1968) The use of the EDL Controlled Reader at Lincoln School. An S.E. Evaluation Report of the Monroe (Michigan) Public Schools.

Hiebert, E. H. (2006). Becoming fluent: Repeated reading with scaffolded texts. In S. J.

Samuels & A. E. Farstrup (Eds.), *What research has to say about fluency instruction* (pp. 204–226). Newark, DE: International Reading Association.

Hoffman, P. A. (1966). Outcomes of controlled reading. *Clearing House, 37,* 90–91.

Honig, B. (1977, September). Reading the right way. *The School Administrator, 8*(54).

Hoover, C. D., & Harris, P. (1997, Winter). The effects of using the ReadFast computer program on eye movement abilities as measured by the OBER2 eye movement device. *Journal of Optometric Vision Development, 28,* 227–234.

Ikeda, M., & Saida, S. (1978). Span of recognition. *Reading Vision Research, 18*(10), 83–88.

James, W. (1890). *Principles of Psychology* (2 Vols.). New York: Henry Holt & Co.

Javal, L. E. (1879, November/December). Essai sur la physiologie de la lecture. *Annales d'oculistique, LXXXII,* 242–253.

Johnson, R., Nottingham, M., Stratton, R., & Zaba, J. N. (1996). The vision screening of academically and behaviorally at-risk pupils. *Journal of Behavioral Optometry, 7*(2), 39–42.

Juel, C. H., & Holmes, B. (1981). Oral and silent reading of sentences. *Reading Research Quarterly, 4,* 545–568.

Kame' enui, E., & Simmons, D. (2001). The DNA reading fluency. *Scientific Studies of Reading, 5*(3), 203–210.

Kennedy, A., & Murray, W. S. (1987a). The components of reading time: Eye movement patterns of good and poor readers. In J. K. O'Regan & A. Levy-Schoen (Eds.), *Eye movements: From physiology to cognition* (pp. 509–520). Amsterdam: North Holland.

Kennedy, A., & Murray, W. S. (1987b). Spatial coordinates and reading: comments on monk. *Quarterly Journal of Experimental Psychology, 39A,* 649–656.

Kennedy, A., & Murray, W. S. (1988). Spatial coding in the processing of anaphor by good and poor readers: Evidence from eye movement analysis. *Quarterly Journal of Experimental Psychology, 40A,* 693–718.

La Berge, D., & Samuels, S. J. (1973). Toward a theory of automatic information processing in reading. *Cognitive Psychology, 6*(2), 293–323.

Logan, G. O. (1997). Automaticity and reading: Perspectives from the instance theory of automaticity. *Reading and Writing Quarterly, 13,* 123–146.

Lyons, G., & Krasnegor, N. (1999). *Attention, memory and executive function.* Baltimore: Paul H. Brooks Publishing Co.

Malone, J. F. (1964). The relative efficiency/controlled reading vs. regular classroom instruction in rate and comprehension with selected eighth grade students. Doctoral Dissertation, University of Texas.

McConkie, G. W., & Rayner, K. (1976). Asymmetry of the perceptual span in reading. *Bulletin of the Psychometric Society, 8,* 365–368.

McConkie, G. W., & Zola, D. (1979). Is visual information integrated across successive fixations in reading? *Perception and Psychophysics, 17,* 578–586.

McConkie, G. W., & Zola, D. (1984, March). Eye movement control during reading: The effect of word units. University of Illinois at Urbana-Champaign Center for the Study of Reading Technical Report.

McDowell, N. A. (1969). Effectiveness of the Controlled Reader in developing reading rates, comprehension and vocabulary as opposed to regular method of testing reading. *Journal of Experimental Education, 32,* 363–369.

McIlvane, W. J., Dube, W. V., & Callahan, T. D. (1999). Attention: A behavior analytical perspective. In G. R. Lyon & N. A. Krasnegor (Eds.), *Attention, memory, and executive function* (2nd printing, pp. 57–70). Baltimore: Paul H. Brookes.

McMahon, M. L. (1956). Development of reading while listening skills in the primary grades. *Reading Research Quarterly, 19*(1), 34 55.

Miller, G. A. (1956). The magic number seven, plus or minus two: Some limits on our capacity for processing information. *Psychological Review, 63,* 81–97.

Mirsky, A. F. (1999). Disorders of attention: A neuropsychological perspective. In G. R. Lyon & N. A. Krasnegor (Eds.), *Attention, memory, and executive function* (2nd printing, pp. 71–96). Baltimore: Paul H. Brookes Publishing Co.

Muller, J. (1826). Zur Vergleichenden Physiologie des Gesichtssinnes des Menschen und der Thiere. Nebst einem Versuch uber die Bewegungen der Augen und uber den menschlichen. Blick, Cnobloch, Leipzig, 251–262.

National Institute of Child Health and Human Development. (2000). Report of the National Reading Panel. Teaching children to read: An evidence-based assessment of the scientific research literature on reading and its implications for reading instruction: Report of the subgroups (NIH Publication No. 00–4769). Washington, DC: U.S. Government Printing Office.

National Parent Teacher Association. (1999, June). Learning related vision problems education and evaluation resolution adopted at the Network PTA Convention.

Neville, M. H. (1975). The effect of rate of aural message on listening and on reading while listening. *Educational Research, 18,* 37–43.

N.Y.S.O.A. Vision Screening Battery Kit. Bernell Corp. www.Bernell.com

O'Connor, R. E., Bell, K. M., Harty, K. R., Larkin, L. K., Sackor, S. M., & Zigmond, N. (2002). Teaching reading to poor readers in the intermediate grades: A comparison of text difficulty. *Journal of Educational Psychology, 94,* 474.

Oller, J., & Jonz, J. (1994). *Cloze and coherence.* New Jersey: Associated University Presses.

Pennington, B. F., Bennetto, L., McNeer, O., & Roberts, R. J., Jr. (1999). *Executive functions and working memory: Attention, memory and executive functions* (pp. 327–348). Baltimore: Paul Brooks Publishing Co.

Pikulski, J. J. (2006). Fluency: A developmental and language perspective. In S. J. Samuels & A. E. Farstrup (Eds.), *What research has to say about fluency instruction* (pp. 70–93). Newark, DE: International Reading Association.

Pinnell, G. S., Pikulski, J. J., Wixson, K. K., Campbell, J. R., Gough, P. B., & Beatty, A. S. Listening to children read aloud. Washington, DC: Office of Educational Research and Improvement, U. S. Department of Education.

Posner, M. I. (1980). Orienting of attention. *Quarterly Journal of Experimental Psychology, 32,* 3–25.

Pressley, M., Gaskins, I. W., & Fingeret, L. (2006). Instruction and development of reading fluency in struggling readers. In S. J. Samuels & A. E. Farstrup (Eds.), *What research has to say about fluency instruction* (pp. 47–69). Newark, DE: International Reading Association.

Punnett, A. F., & Steinhauer, G. D. (1984, May). Relationship between reinforcement and eye movements during ocular-motor training with learning disabled children. *Journal of Learning Disabilities, 17,* 16–19.

Radach, R., Reilly, R., & Inhoff, A. W. (2006). Models of oculomotor control in reading: Towards a theoretical foundation of current debates. In R. van Gompel, M. Fischer, W. Murray, & R. Hill, *Eye movements: A window on mind and brain.* Oxford: Elsevier.

Rashotte, C. A., & Torgesen, J. (1985). Repeated reading and reading fluency in learning disabled children. *Reading Research Quarterly, 12,* 180–188.

Rasinski, T. (1990). Effects of repeated reading and listening-while-reading on reading fluency. *Journal of Educational Research, 83*(3), 147–150.

Rasinski, T. (2006, April). Reading fluency instruction: Moving beyond accuracy, automaticity, and prosody. *The Reading Teacher, 59*(7), 74–76.

Rasinski, T., & Lenhart, L. (2007). Explorations of fluent readers. *Reading Today, 25*(3), 18.

Rasinski, T. V., Reutzel, C. R., Chard, D., & Linan-Thompson, S. (2011). Reading Fluency. In M. L. Kamil, P. D. Pearson, P. Afflerbach, & E. B. Moje (Eds.), *Handbook of Reading Research, IV* (p. 286). New York: Routledge.

Rasinski, T., Samuels, S. J., Hiebert, E., Petscher, Y., & Feller, K. (2011). The relationship between a silent reading fluency instructional protocol on students' reading comprehension and achievement in an urban school setting. *Reading Psychology, 32*(1), 75–97.

Rayner, K. (1983). *Eye movements in reading: Perceptual and language processes.* New York: Academic Press.

Rayner, K., McConkie, K., & Zola, D. (1980). Integrating information across eye-movement. *Cognitive Psychology, 12,* 206–226.

Reitsma, P. (1988). Reading procedure for beginners: Effect of Guided Reading, Reading While Listening and Independent Reading with computer-based speech feedback. *Reading Research Quarterly, 23,* 219–235.

Reutzel, D. R., & Hollingsworth, P. M. (1993). Efforts of fluency training on second graders' reading comprehension. *Journal of Educational Research, 86,* 325–331.

Ruck, W. C. (1982). A program to improve reading skills of mainstream students at the secondary level. School of Education Research Study, Southern Oregon State College.

Rusk, R. R. (1915). A Tachistoscope for class experiment and demonstration purposes. *Journal of Educational Psychology, VI,* 429–431.

Salasoo, A. (1986). Cognitive processing in oral and silent reading comprehension. *Reading Research Quarterly, 21,* 59–69.

Samuels, S. J. (2006). Toward a model of reading fluency. In S. J. Samuels & A. E. Farstrup (Eds.), *What research has to say about fluency instruction* (pp. 24–46). Newark, DE: International Reading Association.

Schlange, D. (1999, December). Evaluation of the Reading Plus 2000 and Visagraph system as a remedial program for academically "at risk" sixth and eighth grade students: A pilot study. Transactions of the Annual Meeting of the American Academy of Optometry, Pediatric Optometry Poster.

Scientific Study of Reading. (2001). Vol. 5, No. 3. Mahwah, NJ: Lawrence Erlbaum Associates.

Seiderman, A. S. (1980, May). Optometric vision therapy: Results of a demonstration project with a learning disabled population. *Journal of the American Optometric Association, 51*(5), 489–493.

Shany, T. M., & Biemiller, A. (1995). Assisted reading practice: Effects on performance for poor readers in grades 3 and 4. *Reading Research Quarterly, 30,* 382–395.

Shelley-Tremblay, J., & Eyer, J. (2009). Effect of the Reading Plus program on reading skills in second graders. *Journal of Behavioral Optometry, 20*(3), 59–66.

Smith, F. (1973). *Understanding Reading.* New York: Holt, Rinehart, & Winston.

Solan, H. A. (1985). Deficient eye-movement patterns in achieving high school students: Three case histories. *Journal of Learning Disabilities, 18*(2).

Solan, H. A. (1987). The improvement of reading efficiency: A study of sixty-three achieving high school students. *Journal of the Reading Specialist,* Vol. 7.

Solan, H. A. (2001, March/April). Role of visual attention in cognitive control of oculomotor readiness in students with reading disabilities. *Journal of Learning Disabilities, 34*(2).

Solan, H. A., Feldman, J., & Tajak, L. (1995). Developing visual and reading efficiency in older adults. *Optometry and Vision Services, 72*(2), 139–148.

Solan, H. A., Larson, S., Shelley-Tremblay, J., Ficcara, A., & Silverman, M. (2001). Role of visual attention in cognitive control of oculomotor readiness in students with reading disabilities. *Journal of Learning Disabilities, 34,* 107–118.

Stahl, S. A., & Kuhn, M. R. (2000). Fluency: A review of developmental and remedial practices. Center for the Improvement of Early Reading Achievement, University of Michigan.

Stahl, S. A., & Kuhn, M. R. (2002). Making it sound like language: Developing fluency. *The Reading Teacher, 55*(6), 582–584.

Stanovich, K. E. (1980). Toward an interactive compensatory model of individual differences in the development of reading fluency. *Research Quarterly, 16*(1), 32–71.

Stanovich, K. E., & Matthew C. (1986). Matthew effects in reading: Some consequences of individual differences in the acquisition of literacy. *Reading Research Quarterly, 21,* 360–406.

Steinman, S., & Steinman, B. (1999, December). Kansas optometric association vision therapy study. Report on data analysis.

Streff, J. W., Poynter, H. L., Jinks, B., & Wolff, B. R. (1990, June). Changes in achievement scores as a result of a joint optometry and education intervention program. *Journal of the American Optometry Association, 61*(65), 475–481.

Taylor, E. A. (1937). *Controlled reading: A correlation of diagnostic, teaching and corrective techniques.* Chicago: University of Chicago Press.

Taylor, S. E. (1964). *Listening. What research says to the teacher, 29.* Washington DC: National Education Association.

Taylor, S. E. (1965). Aural Visual Methods Patent. A patent related to line-by-line presentation of print in coordination with audio pronunciation, 38.

Taylor, S. E. (1976). National study of fluency in the primary grades. Instructional Communications Research Information Brief.

Taylor, S. E. (1976–1978). National study of fluency in the primary grades. Instructional Communications Technology Research and Information Brief.

Taylor, S. E. (1981). National study of fluency in the primary grades, phase II final report–school years 1978–81. Monograph 11, 29. Huntington, New York: Instructional/Communication Technology, Inc.

Taylor, S. E. (2000). Visagraph Eye-Movement Recording System. Taylor Associates.

Taylor, S. E., Frackenpohl, H., & Pettee, J. L. (1960). Grade level norms for the components of the fundamental reading skills. *EDL Research and Information Bulletin, No. 3,* 22. New York: EDL/McGraw Hill.

Taylor, S. E., & Robinson, H. A. (1963). The relationship of the oculomotor efficiency of the beginning reader to his success in learning to read. A paper presented at the American Educational Research Association Conference.

Thompson, V., & Gickling, E. E. (1992, March/April). A personal view of curriculum-based assessment: A response to "critical reflection." *Exceptional Children, 58,* 468–471.

Thompson, W. C. (1956). A book-centered course vs. a machine-centered course: Adult reading improvement. *Journal of Educational Research, 45,* 437–438.

Topping, K. (2006). Building reading fluency: Cognitive, behavioral, and socioemotional factors and the role of peer-mediated learning. In S. J. Samuels & A. E. Farstrup (Eds.), *What research has to say about fluency instruction* (pp. 106–126). Newark, DE: International Reading Association.

Torgesen, J. K., & Hudson, R. F. (2006). Reading fluency: Critical issues for struggling readers. In S. J. Samuels & A. E. Farstrup (Eds.), *What research has to say about fluency instruction* (pp. 130–158). Newark, DE: International Reading Association.

Traxler, A. E. (1935). The relationship between rate of reading and speed of association. *Journal of Educational Psychology,* 357–365.

Van der Leif, A. (1981). Remediation of reading disabled children by presenting text simultaneously to eye and ear. *Bulletin of the Orton Society 31,* 229–243.

Volkmann, A. W. (1859). Das Tachistoskop, ein Instrument, Welches bei Untersuchung des

Momentanen Sehens den Gebrauch de Elektrischens Funkens Ersetzt. Berichte Uber die Verhandlungen der Koniglich Sachischen Gesellschaft der Wissenschaften Zu Leipzig (Math. Phys. Classe). 90–98. (As given by Cassie Spencer Payne).

Wagner, R. K. (1999). From simple structure to complex function: Major trends in the development of theories, models, and measurements of memory. In G. R. Lyon & N. A. Krasnegor (Eds.), *Attention, memory, and executive function* (2nd printing, pp. 139–156). Baltimore: Paul H. Brookes Publishing Co.

Waldstricker, J. S. (1962). Educational rehabilitation and visual education: An interpreted approval. *The Optical Journal and Review of Optometry,* 1–11.

Weber, C. O. (1937). The use of tachistoscopic exercise in the improvement of reading. *Psychological Bulletin, XXXIV,* 533–534.

Wilkins, M. C. (1917). A tachistoscopic experiment in reading. Unpublished master's thesis, Columbia University, 24.

Witzeman, B. E. (1941). An experimental study using the Ophthalm-O-Graph and Metronoscope in the diagnosis and treatment of reading defects. *Journal of Psychology 11,* 307–34.

Yarbus, A. L. (1967). *Eye movements and vision.* New York: Plenum Press.

Chapter 6

TODAY'S TECHNOLOGY TO DEVELOP SILENT READING PROFICIENCY AND FLUENCY

STANFORD E. TAYLOR AND ALEXANDRA SPICHTIG

This chapter will discuss the essential characteristics of a computer software system that is focused on helping students effectively develop high levels of reading proficiency. The instructional techniques of such a system must encompass techniques for student motivation, goal setting, and intensive scaffolded practice to ensure that individual needs are appropriately met as students progress through each step of the system. Proficiency in silent reading necessarily includes the development of fluency or efficiency in silent reading as a first consideration as well as comprehension strategy development and vocabulary enhancement. Fluency in silent reading would be aptly defined as the ability to read with ease and comfort, at adequate reading rates, and with thorough comprehension. Fluency requires high levels of competency in the visual/functional, perceptual, and information processing skills a reader employs to initiate all forms of reading.

The reading proficiency development system described in this chapter could serve as a supplement to core or basal reading programs in grades 1 to 3, since these programs do not presently provide for the development of fluency in silent reading. Such basal programs focus largely on decoding competence, vocabulary introduction, basic comprehension, perhaps the development of oral reading fluency, and an introduction to good literature.

Such a reading proficiency development system can also serve as a supplemental program of reading development in middle and high schools where the development of silent reading proficiency, comprehension competence, and vocabulary enhancement is critical to all learning.

Instructional systems such as *Jamestown Navigator®, Academy of Reading®, Read 180®,* and *Reading Plus®* are presently implemented in many middle and high schools but only Reading Plus®, thus far, provides targeted techniques for the development of fluent and efficient silent reading and contextual analysis skills to enlarge vocabulary.

There are a number of speed-reading programs that purport to develop competency in silent reading as well as very high reading rates. Because the term fluency in silent reading is often associated with both rate of reading and speed reading, it is important to understand the differences between speed reading techniques and fluency development approaches. Some of the more widely publicized speed reading programs include *Speed Your Reading®, Letter Chase Speedreader®, Stretch®, Really Easy Reader®, Rapid Reader®, Speed Reading®, Speed Reading 4 Kids®, SPIDI READ 2007®.*

Most of these programs stress reading rate with minimal or no attention to comprehension skill development and vocabulary improvement. Most require the reader to exert some conscious influence on his or her subliminal visual/perceptual processes during reading (not likely to occur if comprehension is to be maintained). As an example, some programs caution a reader not to regress during reading. Perhaps these programs are able to reduce excessive rereading, but it is unlikely that a reader will be able to sense or control regressions (habitual, reverse fixations or eye stops that last only .24 seconds or less) or eye-movement behavior in general, due to its subliminal nature. Many also claim that their program develops the ability to perceive groups of words within a single eye fixation during continuous reading. This has been disproved; see Chapter 3, Robinson (1934) and Taylor (1957). Some employ single-word or phrase presentations requiring no eye movement as preparation for continuous reading in a left-to-right manner where saccadic movements will typically decrease retention of visual impressions as cited by Gilbert (1959). (See Chapter 5.) Many of these programs also offer left-to-right timed displays of text in some fashion to develop reading rate, but vary in the manner in which portions of print are displayed, seemingly to decrease the number of fixations and regressions that would typically be employed in silent reading.

Many of these speed-reading software programs also stress attaining very high reading rates, above 1,000 words per minute. This is an impossibility when you consider the average adult can move his or her eyes only up to six times per second (approximately 170 ms per eye-stop) and the maximum span of recognition for very advanced readers is only 2.0 to 2.5 words, resulting in a ceiling of about 720 to 900 words per minute. (See Chapter 4.) However, abilities to perceive this maximum number of words per fixation and also utilize the maximum number of fixations per second do not typically occur in concert as documented by E. A. Taylor (1957). Most typically, readers exercising higher than usual spans of recognition will make fewer fixations per second. Thus, it is more reasonable that the usual maximum reading rates for most adults, even after training, will be about 500 to 600 words per minute, as was determined by S. E. Taylor (1962). This is not to say that a few–very few–individuals who possess a photographic memory can read at thousands of words per minute. However, to hold up such a goal for most students is unrealistic.

Skimming and scanning rates are also cited in many of these speed-reading programs. These very high rates, in terms of words dealt with per minute (WDPM) and not words read per minute (WRPM), are achievable, but in skimming and scanning it is presumed that not all the words will be seen or read. This logically brings up the question as to whether all words need to be seen in usual continuous silent reading. For thorough comprehension, all words must be perceived. However, not all words require the same attention during silent reading. A student's level of attention to a particular word will vary based on the importance of the word to comprehension, its familiarity, its orthographic structure, etc.

In summary, most speed-reading courses tend to focus primarily on high rates of reading without enhancement of comprehension or vocabulary development. These courses have not proved to be beneficial according to a study by MacNamara (2000). In addition, Radach, Vorstius, and Reilly (2000) found only a few speed-reading programs that appear to be able to produce some rate improvements in reading. By contrast, a meaningful and comprehensive reading proficiency development program must be practical in terms of the many goals that can be achieved by students with various learning needs and backgrounds.

When considering what comprises a comprehensive approach to reading proficiency development, there are many facets of training and practice to consider. According to Rasinski, Samuels, Hiebert, Petscher, and Feller (2011), some key characteristics of a successful reading proficiency program that develops fluency in silent reading would include:

1. Assigning proper level of reading content for each student to ensure success in reading practice, thus increasing motivation to read more.
2. Scheduling a reasonable amount of silent reading practice per week. Rasinski, Samuels, Hiebert, Petscher, and Feller (2011) referred to a Miami study in which 90 minutes per week was cited as producing good progress and success. By contrast, core reading programs scheduled only 50 minutes or less per week per individual student.
3. Scaffolding instruction appropriately to accommodate individual students' levels of competence and progress.

4. Adequate supervision of reading practice, either through teacher monitoring or computer progress reports.

While most everyone agrees with the above cited requirements, the authors of this chapter also believe it is essential for a comprehensive approach to determine how students process text, which includes the most basic visual/functional, perceptual, and information processing skills that initiate all forms of reading It is evident that the efficiency of these skills must first be evaluated. Today, this can be done effectively and easily through eye-movement recording, which can document precisely "how" a student reads, and his or her need for development of these types of basic skills, and, ultimately, the gains made through training in these skills. This appraisal information, when combined with other diagnostic and norm or criteria reference test results, will provide a more complete picture of a student's reading achievement or proficiency as well as the types and qualities of his or her learning needs.

Reading/Vocabulary Assessment

The first step in an effective instructional program is the administration of a reading proficiency assessment to establish each student's current proficiency level and learning needs, and place the student in appropriate practice level content. A comprehension appraisal can be administered in a lab or classroom (as shown in the following image) to a number of students simultaneously to save time.

Step 1: Obtaining a Tentative Independent Reading Level

In an initial proficiency assessment, students should be given a series of short reading selections, starting at what is presumed to be their independent reading level. These selections might be 100–200 words in length (ranging in reading level 1–12) that are followed by literal recall questions to determine the student's ability to capture the information read. Although the reading selection displayed may be timed, students should be allowed to move forward at their own pace by moving from screen to screen whenever they are finished reading. A student's reading rate for each selection would be recorded for later analysis.

In this fashion, students would progress from very easy content to higher and more difficult or perhaps easier content based on comprehension scores. Students might start their reading three levels below grade level, or perhaps lower if their true level of independent reading is judged to be below this level. As students progress through the reading selections and complete comprehension questions, the end result would be to determine the highest level at which a student can read independently with reasonable rates and acceptable comprehension.

Step 2: Confirming the Independent Practice Level

Next, a longer selection, perhaps 300–500 words or more in length, should be read, to confirm the findings of the assignment in Step 1 when more reading stamina and more extensive comprehension are required. This selection would likely need to be at a student's tentative independent reading level as determined by Step 1. The reading of this longer selection would be followed by more diverse comprehension questions involving higher level thinking skills (i.e., inference, main idea) that demonstrate a deeper level of comprehension. Comprehension performance will either confirm the tentative assignment of independent reading level as determined by Step 1, or identify a more appropriate lower independent reading level. Again, comprehension and reading rate performances should be considered in establishing a student's true independent reading level.

Step 3: Determining a Vocabulary Study Level

A vocabulary assessment should be administered to determine a student's instructional needs and appropriate placement within vocabulary development programs. Multiple choice questions may be used to elicit such information. The assessment might start at the reading level determined by Step 2. And, since vocabulary study levels are typically one to two levels higher than a student's independent reading level, he or she will most likely progress upward several levels in the vocabulary assessment before making a significant number of errors on a level. When significant errors are made on a level, this vocabulary study level might be assigned.

Step 4: Ascertaining Readiness to Perceive Words with Accuracy

Should a student exhibit difficulty with the lowest reading level content (1.5 readability), a perceptual memory appraisal should be automatically provided. Such an appraisal would determine a student's readiness for word recognition and decoding instruction through exercises that ask for the identification of letters, short words, and then slightly longer words. Teachers may also elect to employ such an appraisal with students before they engage in the reading appraisal, as described in Step 1, if they suspect that a student will experience difficulty with first grade content.

Step 5: Testing Competence in Decoding

If a student struggles with primary grade content, then a decoding test might be administered. Such a vocabulary test would desirably involve the pronunciation of letter clusters in words as a student pronounces target letter clusters. Progress is being made in voice recognition that very soon should permit this form of appraisal.

Step 6: Assessing Visual/Functional, Perceptual and Information Processing Efficiency

After a reading and vocabulary appraisal is completed to determine the best level of content for reading proficiency development, it is recommended that an eye-movement recording appraisal be administered to evaluate the visual/functional, perceptual, and information processing efficiency of a student when reading appropriate level content. (See the following image.) The level of the test selection should match a student's independent reading level as identified by Step 2. There is a need to examine more specifically "how" a student reads easy-to-read content. This form of appraisal is useful in confirming that the initial practice level assigned is appropriate, by identifying reading efficiency characteristics and text processing habits that may impact reading instructional scheduling decisions and to suggest differentiated instructional approaches. Eye movement recording also provides a valuable means of evaluating fluency development progress from time to time.

As stated in Chapter 2, an excessive number of fixations and regressions as well as a prolonged duration of fixation could signal a lack of instant word recognition and, depending on the severity, may cause a reconsideration of the assigned practice level, a practice regimen, or simply suggest the need for more frequent scheduling of fluency practice sessions per week as well as a longer or shorter overall schedule of training. A slow rate of reading in accordance with other performance measures may indicate inadequate input into short-term memory, which might cause a reconsideration of increases in reading rate (small, medium, or large) to be used in the timed and scanned guided reading lessons to follow. Likewise, difficulty in directional attack could also indicate a less than desirable recognition of words or sequence of word input into short-term memory, which might signal the need to assign more than the usual number of timed and left-to-right guided reading lessons to ensure more rapid development of a good directional attack.

Beyond these suggestions that could affect the nature of the practice to be assigned, the visual/functional reports that evaluate competency of binocular coordination, could signal the need for a student to engage in home study visual training practice or be examined by a vision specialist in order to ensure that poor visual skills will not impede progress in a reading efficiency program.

An appropriate appraisal that includes Steps 1 through 6 will provide a teacher with a more complete picture of a student's level of reading proficiency and instructional needs.

After a placement appraisal such as the one just described has been completed, students will be placed in appropriate level practice content. Students will then engage in a reading proficiency development program that encompasses structured, adaptive, and differentiated fluency development, comprehension building, and vocabulary expansion. (See the following diagram.)

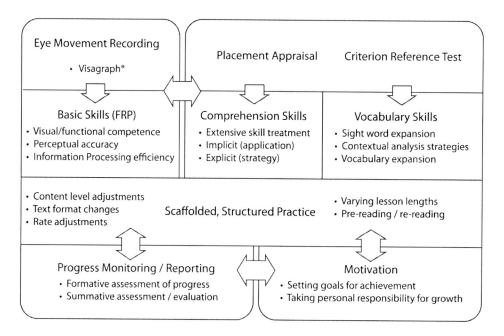

A primary consideration is the development of the basic skills of visual, perceptual, and information processing. The development of these skills must be provided in a scaffolded manner to provide the most appropriate instruction and practice for each individual. Content difficulty choices should be guided by a student's current ability level in terms of his or her vocabulary knowledge, comprehension proficiency and rate of reading. The length of reading selections should also be varied to accommodate a student's level of reading stamina and attention. Reading selections should be presented in ways that most effectively interact with a reader's need for structure and guidance. Text may be presented in a variety of display formats, such as full page, guided reading[1] in a timed and left-to-right scrolled display manner,

---

1. In this chapter and in previous chapters, the term guided reading will be used to describe a timed left-to-right display of text. This term has evolved from the use of the Guided Read™, a device used in the 1980s to develop fluency in silent reading. Today, many educators also use the term "guided reading" to describe teacher-directed small-group reading enhancement activities.

line-by-line, or word-by-word, depending on a student's perceptual and/or comprehension needs. Presentation rates must be in accordance with a student's proficiency level to ensure satisfactory comprehension. Finally, pre-reading as well as rereading activities should be employed to ensure students develop effective comprehension strategies that assist in satisfactory meaning gathering from text at reading rates that are realistic and maintainable.

Comprehension skill enhancement must be constantly stressed to develop competency in all of the major cognitive areas such as the ones proposed by Bloom's Taxonomy (1956) as well as L. W. Anderson (2001) that prepare students for college and career demands in an inclusive manner. Comprehension development opportunities may be provided in various forms. An implicit or integrated series of comprehension checks may be used along with each reading lesson to provide students with opportunities to demonstrate the extent of their comprehension of what was read. Teacher-directed single-skill lessons may also be used to provide explicit comprehension strategy instruction and application. Vocabulary development may be needed for some students to build their capacity in sight word recognition as well as general vocabulary use and knowledge. Further, there must be a provision for the development of contextual strategies that will facilitate a student's capability to elicit the meaning of less familiar words during continuous reading.

Beyond the inclusion of practice techniques, a comprehensive system must provide continuous progress reports to students, parents/guardians, teachers, and administrators. Every instructional program requires careful monitoring of use as well as achievement to be successful.

Reports will also serve as great motivation for students to set goals and achieve them. Program progress is key to continued student application and will play a vital role in developing a student's personal responsibility for their growth and achievement.

Fluency, Comprehension and Vocabulary Instruction

Fluency in silent reading, good comprehension, and a broad vocabulary are the three major components of reading proficiency as stated in previous chapters. Each has been the subject of extensive research, and each should be addressed by various components in a comprehensive reading proficiency development program.

Rasinski (2006) stated:

> The link between fluency and overall reading proficiency is now well established. Several reviews of research related to reading fluency have come to this conclusion (Chard, Vaughn, & Tyler, 2002; Dowhower, 1994; Kuhn & Stahl, 2000; NICHD, 2000; Rasinski & Hoffman, 2003; Strecker, Roser, &

Martinez, 1998). Nevertheless, our understanding of reading fluency and its place in the reading process and reading curriculum is far from complete. (p. 18)

A key focus of a reading proficiency development program is the achievement of fluency in silent reading. What is believed to comprise fluency in silent reading will vary from researcher to researcher but, in summary, these are the proficiencies that seem to be agreed upon by most as required for fluency in silent reading to emerge:

- focused and sustained attention
- competent visual coordination and proper print perception
- fully developed orthographic competencies
- automaticity of word recognition
- rapidity of word association or phrasing
- effective use of short- and long-term memory
- adequate reading vocabulary
- competency in employing a wide variety of comprehension strategies
- achievement of adequate silent reading rates.

When students are accomplished in these skill areas, they will be able to read at adequate rates with thorough comprehension and in a manner that facilitates ease and comfort. However, attaining adequate levels of fluency is an ongoing process through the grades. As students move up in reading levels, they will encounter more difficult vocabulary to master, more demanding content, the need for more advanced comprehension strategies, vocabulary expansion, and the requirement for increased reading rates that are suitable for each new level of reading and study tasks.

Focused and Sustained Attention

Attention is the acquired ability to focus the mind on a single activity or concept as described in Chapter 5. It can either be consciously, voluntarily directed, or involuntarily attracted. Thus, a first consideration of a reading proficiency program would be to engage students and involve them in a manner that will help develop the capacity for sustained attention.

Students could start each computerized training session with a visual and perceptual "warm-up" such as scan and flash activities with numbers and letters, which are both motivating and challenging. These activities also require exacting scrutiny of the target numbers and/or letters to which students are exposed, which will develop orthographic competence, improved visual coordination, and the use of a strong visual memory. Further, the task of retaining the number or letter combinations that are flashed requires intense concentration in order to retain accuracy of perception.

In scan training a target number or letter is assigned and students count the appearance of this element as the letters or numbers are displayed from left to right at speeds ranging from 30 lines per minute to 120 lines per minute. (See the following example.)

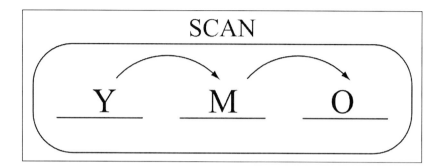

After scan training flash practice may also be provided. During flash, exposures of numbers or letters are presented at one-sixth of a second and then students type in what they can retain. They are then corrected if there are errors. (See the following example.)

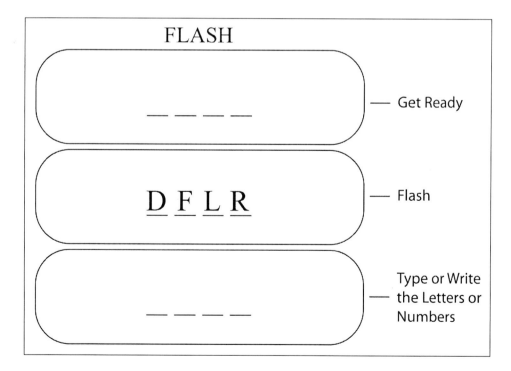

Following this initial visual and perceptual "warm-up," a guided reading lesson, which provides visually guided displays of text, will require that students use those same high-attention levels in reading a selection to develop fluency in silent reading. To start, students may engage in keyword activities to ensure familiarity with key words that are important to the understanding of the story. The words would be flashed and typed, which requires initial focus. Then, the reading selection is presented in a timed and left-to-right scanned fashion, as shown in the following display, at appropriately calibrated rates. This guided approach to reading helps develop improved tracking, automaticity of word recognition, and improved reading rates. This paced presentation of text will require that students maintain a high level of attention and concentration for a reasonable interval of time, perhaps 8 to 10 minutes of reading. One of the goals of such training is also to develop higher levels of reading stamina.

the largest car-racing

Adequate Visual Coordination

As described in Chapter 5, it is important to realize that the near-point activity of reading is not a natural human act. However, all students must accomplish the necessary visual adjustments for close work in order to become fluent readers. (See the following illustration.)

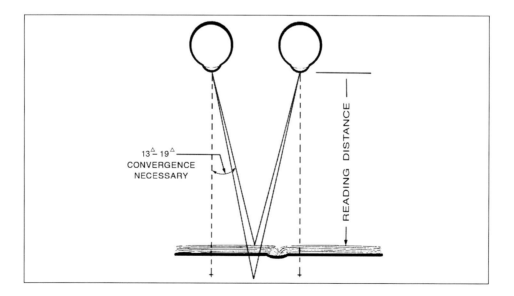

The College of Optometrists in Vision Development (COVD) posted this statement on their website (www.covd.org):

> "A learning-related visual problem directly affects
> how we learn, read, or sustain close work."

It is essential that students maintain good binocular coordination and vergence (team use of both eyes), possess acceptable ocular motility (the ability to rotate the eyes and not the head), and track accurately (staying on the line and progressing sequentially across lines of print with good left-to-right directional attack). If a student does not have good visual/functional skills, reading will not be a comfortable activity, and this can cause poor attention and concentration. Further, poor visual skills can cause a student to see print in a blurred or muddy fashion, interfering with accuracy of word recognition. Stated simply, if the student cannot function well visually, it is unlikely that fluency in silent reading will emerge.

Exercises involving scanning of numbers and letters and subsequent guided reading training activities that employ timed left-to-right scanning of text will improve visual tracking and encourage better binocular coordination as shown by Hellerstein et al. (2001), Hoover and Harris (1997), and Schlange (1999). As students learn to track more accurately across lines at higher and higher rates, their ocular motility improves (head movement replaced by movement of the eyes) and their ability to use both eyes as a team will be enhanced. This reading training is not to be construed as a replacement for vision training that can be provided by a qualified vision specialist for those requiring this type of intervention. It may well be assumed that up to 5 to 8 percent of students in any given school or district will benefit from additional professional vision training. These students, needing such intensive visual training, may be easily detected through Visagraph® eye-movement recordings.

There are also home study visual training activities such as those provided for in the Taylor Associates EyesPlus program that can help many students who are marginal in terms of their need for improvement of binocular coordination. (See http://www.readingplus.com/eyesplus.)

Fully Developed Orthographic Competencies

Students need to become skilled in the most basic word identification skills in terms of recognizing letters and letter order in words. They need to be able to instantly and accurately recognize the orthographic structure of words, which they will later identify as a given word and then proceed to word association.

According to Pikulski (2006):

> According to Ehri (1995, 1998), careful processing of print in the fully alphabetic stage leads to this rapid, instant recognition. Partial alphabetic readers store incomplete representations of words and, therefore, confuse similar words such as were, where, wire, and wore.

Whether words are recognized as sight words or decoded through phonetic analysis, it is essential that the letter order configuration is accurately perceived. Identifying the letter and letter order of words is quite trainable. Not only does developing orthographic accuracy aid the development of instant word recognition, but it also facilitates improved spelling abilities, which are also quite dependent on visual memory.

Through scan and flash activities, students can quickly and easily develop the capacity to identify letters and numbers accurately and in proper sequence. In flash exposures of numbers or letters, at one-sixth of a second, students get only one glimpse (during one fixation) of a letter configuration, for there is no time to move their eyes. Thus, they develop the ability to accurately identify the elements flashed and their sequential order within a single fixation.

Additionally, word recognition practice with scanning, flashing, and typing of words can provide continued orthographic recognition training with core high frequency vocabulary words, as compiled by Taylor in 1989, all of the 2007 Dolch core vocabulary, as well as the Zeno et al. (1995) high frequency word list.

Automaticity of Word Recognition

Researchers today agree that automaticity, or instant recognition of words, is vital if a student is to be able to focus on understanding what is read, and that automaticity in word recognition is a key requirement for fluency in reading to emerge. Adams (1994) stated, "If it takes a child too long to identify successive words, the beginning of the sentence will fade from memory before the end has been registered" (p. 857). If word recognition and comprehension both require conscious attention, one or the other or both will suffer.

In their classic article, LaBerge and Samuels (1974) stated, "At the accuracy level of performance, attention is assumed to be necessary for processing; at the automatic level it is not."

Scan and flash exposures with core vocabulary will develop word recognition automaticity. During scan training a student must count the number of times a target word appears as words are displayed from 50 to 280 words per minute, as depicted in the illustration that follows.

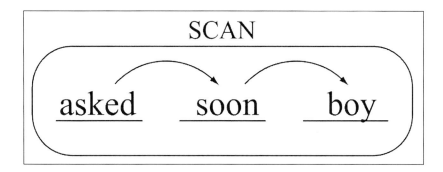

After scan training, flash practice with a series of words can heighten word recognition automaticity. During flash training words are exposed at one-sixth of a second timed intervals. After the flashing of each word, the student will type in the word. A repeat flash should be available for students, and students should not be able to type incorrect letters. (See the following example.)

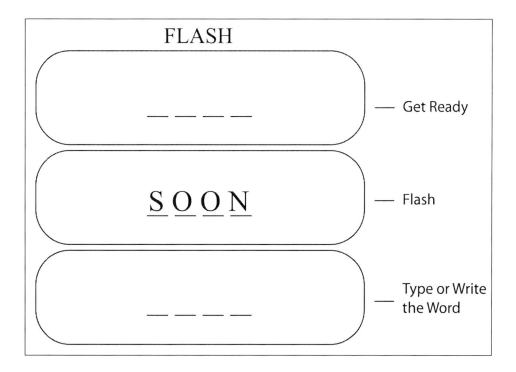

When the words are flashed, a student must perceive the total word in a single fixation, for there is no time for a second fixation. Thus, a student will be encouraged to perceive words in a single visual fixation and in far less time than in the usual duration of fixation during continuous reading, leaving time for word association.

Later, in a guided reading program, keywords to be encountered in reading a selection will first be flashed in context, and students will type in these words. Then the narrator would pronounce these words. This preparatory word recognition training will prepare students to more instantly recognize these words accurately as they are encountered while reading the selection. Then, as students read the selection in timed and left-to-right displays of reading content they will again encounter these words, but they will not need to depart from fluent reading to decode. At the same time, fluency in silent reading requires some risk taking in which students try to do the best they can with word recognition, and proceed to realize phrasing and complete meaning. During guided reading, core or high-frequency vocabulary should be repeated again and again throughout the selections. This repetition of vocabulary will also contribute greatly to more instant sight word recognition, and since students are being assessed on comprehension after each lesson, it is assured they will be learning more than word-calling skills.

Rapidity of Word Association or Phrasing

Students need to be able to rapidly assimilate and associate individual words during their reading and thus recognize familiar speech phrasing that will lead to a better understanding of the meaning of sentences they read. Rasinski (2006) reported:

Rasinski (1990) performed a review of research conducted over several decades related to instruction focused on text phrasing. The results of the review suggested that a focus on phrasing has substantial potential for delivering positive outcomes across a number of areas related to reading proficiency. (p. 16)

Oral reading in the early grades can certainly contribute to a student's awareness of phrasing, but in later grades, a student needs to realize phrases by rapidly recognizing and associating words in proper sequence. The configuration of words perceived and word association, in terms of the meaning expressed by a phrase, lags behind the visual intake of words, as cited in Chapter 5. Wagner (1999) reinforced this concept, "Presumably the contents of short-term memory would lag behind the eyes with a three- to four-word delay corresponding to the eye-voice span" (p. 144).

Thus a more rapid and sequential input of words into short-term memory can enhance the potential for word association, phrasing, and increased understanding of what has been read.

Beyond the reading of guided reading selections to enhance word association and phrasing competence, a timed and scanned training could be provided with phrased content if a student appears to be experiencing excessive difficulty with literal comprehension in grades 1 to 3.

Effective Use of Short- and Long-Term Memory

Wagner (1999) defined short-term memory as follows; "Short-term memory is best conceptualized as that portion of long-term memory that is temporarily at a heightened state of activation at a particular moment in time." He went on to discuss two key characteristics of short-term memory. "First, short-term memory is not a separate, dedicated storage area. . . ." and "Second, the capacity for short-term storage is limited, which is implied by the idea that the heightened state of activation of a given portion of long-term memory is temporary," as also cited by Shiffrin, Ratcliff, Murnane, and Nobel, 1993 (p. 148), and Cowan, 1993 (p. 166).

As students read along lines of print, the word data is first input into short-term memory, and then long-term memory is activated to assist in comprehension. In order for this to happen effectively, word input into short-term memory must be rapid, sequential, and coherent; otherwise, students will have to divert their processing faculties to decode, decipher, and reorganize the word data, which will delay comprehension and understanding.

Miller (1956) concluded that only about seven items (plus or minus two) can be stored in short-term memory before the earliest items would begin to fade. Further, time in seconds is also a constraint on what can be retained in short-term memory as stated by Broadbent (1975). This time ranges from 3 to 20 seconds.

What constitutes an item? Broadbent (1975) and Cowan (2001) concluded that three to four units was the maximum. One might logically conclude that, in reading, a word would be the smallest item stored in short-term memory. But what happens when a reader makes several fixations to perceive a word? It may well be that each of these individual visual impressions may constitute separate items and that long-term memory must be drawn upon to recode or reorganize these impressions into the recognition of a single word, which then becomes a single item. Certainly the realization of phrases (chunking of words) reduces the number of items to be stored in short-term memory. Chunking will facilitate the use of long-term memory in its translation of this information into an awareness of the meaning of a sentence and, at the same time, will confirm the meaning or use of the component words in the sentence.

Guided reading fluency practice, encourages a reader to input words into short-term memory rapidly and in proper sequence, which will facilitate word association and comprehension. The linguistic and conceptual patterns in long-term memory, stored from prior reading, learning, and life experiences, will then be effectively engaged, aiding, consolidating, and deepening understanding of what has been read. As students achieve accurate literal understanding through effective use of short-term memory, they will be able to draw on comprehension strategies stored in the metacognitive areas of long-term memory to interpret, analyze, evaluate, and eventually appreciate the content they have read.

Reading Vocabulary

It is evident that students need to amass a larger instant sight vocabulary if they are to achieve fluency. Torgesen and Hudson (2006) cited an older study when they said:

> In an earlier analysis (Torgesen, Rashotte, & Alexander, 2001), we provided substantial evidence that the single most important factor in accounting for individual differences in reading fluency among students with reading disabilities was the speed with which individual words are recognized. (p. 140)

What words to address becomes the next question. Hiebert (2006) reported:

> It has long been recognized that a relatively small number of words accounts for a substantial percentage of total words encountered in reading (Thorndike, 1921). Based on a sample of 17.25 million words in texts used from kindergarten through college, Zeno, Ivens, Millard, and Duvvuri (1995) reported that 25 words account for 33% of the total words in the corpus. When the number of different words gets to around 5,575, approximately 90% of the total words in texts from third through ninth grade (Carroll et al., 1971) and about 80% of the total words in texts from kindergarten through college (Zeno et al., 1995) are accounted for. (p. 209)

Beyond the repetition and reinforcement of high frequency vocabulary–which is the first step in reading vocabulary development–extensive reading is an obvious requirement. As students read extensively in a wide variety of genres, their vocabulary will be greatly expanded. Beyond these two basic vocabulary considerations, there is also the need to engage students in contextual analysis cloze activities, which will result in a more widely developed capacity to discover the meaning and use of words as they read through an examination of the words in the sentences or paragraphs in which they appear. The majority of the vocabulary to be used in an ideal software program would be taken from high frequency, core-vocabulary lists.

Ensuring Comprehension in Silent Reading

Fluency in silent reading implies good comprehension. Rate, with less than adequate comprehension, is meaningless. As a consequence, any silent reading fluency development program must contain a wide variety of comprehension building activities that will ensure thorough comprehension. Some of the areas of student engagement previously mentioned with regard to focused and sustained attention, improvement of visual coordination, development of orthographic competence, automaticity of word recognition, and more rapid word association, as well as more effective use of short-term memory are basic to good comprehension. Other critical areas of consideration are:

- Reading appropriate level content
- Pre-reading preparation activities
- Extensive Reading
- Skill-based comprehension questions
- Directed skill reinforcement lessons
- Writing activities
- Semantic mapping lessons

Reading Appropriate Level Content

Students can most effectively develop efficient and thorough comprehension skills during silent reading if they start their silent reading practice at their independent reading level. Thus it is essential to use a reading placement appraisal that identifies an appropriate start level at which students can demonstrate satisfactory comprehension in accordance with reasonable reading rates. As students develop in terms of their capacity to relate information and achieve good comprehension over a number of lessons, they can be moved to higher levels of content and greater comprehension challenges.

Betts (1946) stated that about one word per hundred should be a difficult one in independent reading. If the number of less-recognizable words is too great, a reader will be encouraged to depart from fluent silent reading and engage in decoding, thus reducing the potential for silent reading fluency development.

According to Pressley, Gaskins, and Fingeret (2006), "The best text for aiding struggling readers to become fluent readers appears to be those that have a controlled vocabulary consisting of a high percentage of both high-frequency words and words with consistent and decodable patterns."

Prereading Preparation Activities

A series of studies by Duffy, Sherman, and Roehler (1977) demonstrated that students can learn to be strategic readers. Preparation activities prior to reading can obviously help students develop reading strategies and purposes for reading that will improve their comprehension.

In KEEP, the Kamehaneha elementary program, as discussed by Tharp (1982), teachers relied heavily on a variety of levels of questions and discussions for comprehension building. The basic goal in this extensive guided practice was to answer a variety of questions that would help students improve their performance on comprehension tests.

Other examples could involve teacher/student group discussions. However, in the case of individualized computer lessons, presenting students with statements or questions concerning a reading lesson to follow provides a unique opportunity to prepare students for their reading. Such preparation may include questions, eliciting student assumptions, or simple statements that suggest a picture of the story. Samples of such statements or questions that might be posed prior to reading a selection might be as follows:

Running With the Dogs
- What is sled-dog racing?
- What type of person races sled dogs?
- What does it take in terms of preparation and skill?
- How does someone get started in racing sled dogs?

Space Camp
- A place where campers can experience what it is like to travel in space
- The origins of a Space Camp
- What campers do at Space Camp

Extensive Reading

Getting students to read more extensively and independently is also key to developing their proficiency in reading. Allington (2006) stated, "The intervention I would propose is straightforward. Provide these children with high-success reading experiences all day long." In regard to extensive reading, students need to be exposed to a wide variety of interesting genres in their reading practice to develop the capability of reading flexibly. They need to encounter different types of writing and varying topics to develop the capacity to read a wide variety of content in both their subject area studies and general reading.

More varied reading always results in better readers. An effective reading development fluency system will provide extensive practice lessons in a wide variety of interesting and engaging genres such as history and biography, science and nature, life skills and career, classics and contemporary fiction, family and relationships, sports and leisure, and travel and culture as depicted in the following visual.

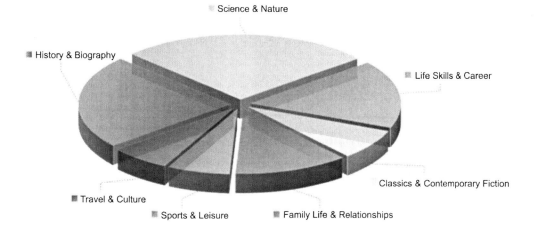

Table 6.1 shows the progression of narratives versus informational texts through the levels, as proposed by the 2009 reading framework of the National Assessment of Educational Progress (NAEP). Thus it is critical to also align instructional material with such a framework to ensure more students are better prepared to tackle assessment texts. At each level there should be extensive practice lessons in a wide variety of content at each student's own independent reading level.

Table 6.1

Grade Level	Literary Texts	Informational Texts
4	50%	50%
8	45%	55%
12	30%	70%

Skill-Based Comprehension Questions

Many researchers suggest that students will learn a particular cognitive process by answering questions related to that process after reading a selection. Pearson and Gallagher (1983) and their colleagues conducted a series of studies in which students also benefited from explicit comprehension instruction. It seems logical then that students need experience with a wide variety of types of comprehension questions following their reading to broaden the scope of the comprehension skills they can employ as they read a wide variety of content.

A comprehensive reading development program should involve practice with skill-based questions in the following five major areas:

1. Literal Understanding
- Recalling Information and Details
- Following Sequence of Ideas or Events
- Identifying Speaker

2. Interpretation
- Determining Main Idea
- Making Inferences
- Predicting Outcomes
- Drawing Conclusions
- Interpreting Figurative Language
- Visualizing
- Paraphrasing

3. Analysis
- Comparing and Contrasting
- Recognizing Cause and Effect
- Classifying
- Reasoning
- Identifying Analogies

4. Evaluation
- Detecting Author's Purpose
- Understanding Persuasion
- Recognizing Slant and Bias
- Distinguishing between Fact and Opinion
- Judging Validity
- Determining Relative Importance

5. Appreciation
- Interpreting Character
- Recognizing Emotional Reactions

- Identifying Mood and Tone
- Identifying Setting

These skills follow Bloom's Taxonomy as updated by Anderson and Krathwohl (2001), (see the following diagram), which embrace the full range of lower- to higher-order thinking skill demands:

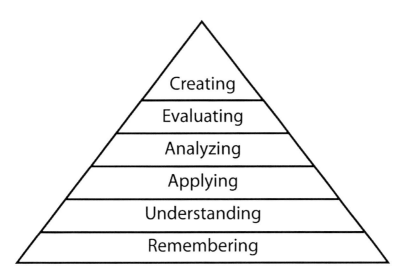

Directed Skill Reinforcement Lessons

If a student experiences consistent difficulties in answering a certain type of comprehension skill question, providing specific single skill instruction in that particular form of cognitive activity will allow students to internalize this comprehension process for use in later reading. Not only should they understand the process, but they should also have practice in applying that comprehension skill in practice exercises. Applying the skill ensures that the cognitive process is truly understood and can be used in the future.

Students will need to be able to engage in these skill lessons at their appropriate reading level. These lessons can be presented by the teacher as small-group lessons (using a particular skill lesson that is at the lowest reading level of the group) or as independent skill-development lessons. Even more competent readers can profit from easy-to-understand explicit comprehension skill lessons.

As students complete these individualized skill lessons, they will internalize the cognitive process treated for later use in global, inductive reading.

Writing Activities

It is recommended that students engage in writing activities that allow them to use and extend the information they encountered in a given reading lesson. Writing gives students an opportunity to relate to the information they read by extending their focus beyond what was stated in terms of using judgment, evaluation, and appreciation.

Writing prompts may be of a journaling nature stimulating creative writing or involve a direct skill target allowing students to exercise a particular type of thinking skill or sub-skill. Following are some examples of such writing prompts:

Creative Writing Prompts:

- What steps would you take to develop a community garden where you live?
- Do you think bird feeding should be discouraged? If not, why? If so, how could this be done?
- If you had a camera, what would you like to photograph? What would you do with your photographs?
- Have you ever had to overcome problems to achieve a goal? How did you do it?
- Dogs are an important part of the sport of dog-sled racing. What other sports or hobbies involve dogs in some way?

Skill Focused Writing Prompts:

- Compare how two characters from stories that you have read are similar to each other or contrast how they are different from each other.
- Provide an example from the story of "false cause." Demonstrate that because one event follows another does not prove that the second event is caused by the first event.
- How would you apply what you learned in the story you read to your own life?
- Did the author of the story have first-hand knowledge about the subject presented? If yes, explain how you can tell. If no, explain how first-hand knowledge might change the author's perspective.

Adequate Silent Reading Rates

According to Rasinski and Lenhart (2007), "Reading rate (how fast one reads) seems to have emerged as the key defining characteristic of reading fluency, and fluency has come to be assessed through measurements of reading rate" (p. 18). Obviously, rate and comprehension have to function together. Rate without good comprehension is meaningless. Thus, fluency in silent reading means adequate reading rate, good comprehension, as well as ease and comfort in reading. See the norm reading rates in Table 6.2.

Table 6.2

Taylor National Norms												
Grade Level	1	2	3	4	5	6	7	8	9	10	11	12
Norm Rates	80	115	138	158	173	185	195	204	214	224	237	250
Target Rates	140	170	200	230	250	270	280	300	310	325	345	365

These norm rates are simply usual grade level rates, and so it is expected that target reading rates after a fluency development program would be much higher than norm rates as shown in Table 6.2.

As an example of the need for higher rates, consider that beginning readers should logically achieve reading rates between 125 and 175 wpm, which would return their reading performances to their usual listening and speaking communication rates, as cited by Taylor (1964).

Beyond this, in the intermediate grades it seems reasonable to expect silent reading rates to be above 200 wpm if students are to reduce the tendency to vocalize and to read more effectively and silently in their content area studies.

At the secondary and college levels, the nature of assigned reading would seem to require that students accomplish reading rates of 300–400 wpm or higher to complete their studies in a reasonable period of time.

In a guided reading program, text presentation rates would be directly affected by a student's comprehension performance. Students' comprehension performance would be used to initially calibrate an individualized presentation start rate as well as to continuously monitor and adjust presentation rates throughout the intervention period. Rate adjustments may be modest, average, or more aggressive based on an analysis of a student's comprehension performance pattern, rate performance pattern, milestone achievement and so forth. At various time intervals, rates may be stabilized momentarily or for longer periods of time, to allow a student to practice and stabilize rate gains. As students qualify to move to a higher level of content, the rate may be recalibrated, adjusted, stabilized as needed to meet student needs at this higher level.

SCAFFOLDING OF INSTRUCTION

At times, students may respond somewhat differently in silent reading development with regard to attention span, comprehension, reading rate increases, etc. An "intelligent" scaffolding system must be employed that will sense the nature of student progress and alter reading level content, lesson presentation formats, rate of text presentation, repeat and pre-reading assignments, etc., to automate instruction in order to maximize comprehension and progress. Some examples of scaffolding changes that might be made are as follows:

- Content level may be adjusted to provide easier content.
- Lesson formats may be adjusted to provide support mechanisms that accommodate a student's current reading stamina as well as guide him or her to higher performance levels.
- Various degrees of structure (i.e., partially guided to fully guided presentation modes) may be used to provide students with necessary support mechanisms to develop efficient reading habits, break through rate, plateaus, or simply eliminate bad habits.
- Repeat readings with additional questions may be assigned to strengthen comprehension.
- Prereading activities may be used to assist students in accommodating to rate increases without compromising comprehension.
- Rate stabilization phases may be implemented to allow students to better acclimate to higher reading rates.

Such automatic scaffolding changes along with teacher notifications that may prompt student observation and/or conferences are vital components of an automated management system monitoring reading practice for each student.

While such adjustments in practice have been made by teachers in the past, automatic scaffolding of instruction should, today, be part of any computerized silent reading fluency development system to maximize student progress as such adjustments can be executed promptly and continuously and allow for teacher time to be spent more profitably on targeted teacher-student interaction and motivation.

REPORTS AND MOTIVATION

Progress reports about rate and comprehension are essential if students are to be adequately motivated to take responsibility for their own progress.

Such reports are also essential from the standpoint of the teacher, who must constantly monitor student progress and be able to spend appropriate time with students who demonstrate the need for additional intervention strategies, more motivation and better application. The administrator also must review progress reports to be assured that the proper gains are being made that will lead to higher state and standardized test scores.

Further, an effective reading proficiency development program must, at intervals, reward students for good achievement. Progress certificates might be generated automatically to acknowledge those students who are making good progress. Letting students see their progress is a great step toward encouraging them to take responsibility for their own learning.

FLEXIBILITY IN READING

Once students in grade 4 and higher have acquired reasonable levels of fluency or efficiency in silent reading, they need to develop competency in other study skill reading approaches. If a Visagraph® eye-movement recording device is available, the level of efficiency in reading grade level content with satisfactory comprehension would be evident in terms of the number of fixations, regressions, duration of fixation, and reading rate. It is essential that fluency or efficiency be the first consideration that will qualify students to move on to developing flexibility with different study skill approaches. Beyond fluency or efficiency in usual reading, as in guided reading, there is accelerated reading, critical or study type reading, and skimming and scanning to be mastered. Guided reading prepares a student in terms of developing efficiency with basic visual/perceptual skills to be able to "shift gears" in reading and allow the development of competence in these other forms of reading approaches. (See the following diagram.)

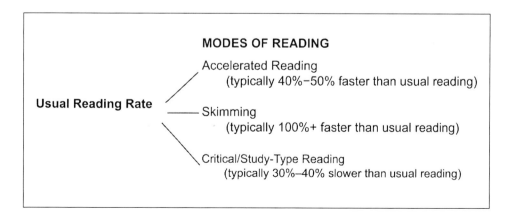

MODES OF READING

Usual Reading Rate

Accelerated Reading
(typically 40%–50% faster than usual reading)

Skimming
(typically 100%+ faster than usual reading)

Critical/Study-Type Reading
(typically 30%–40% slower than usual reading)

ACCELERATED READING

Accelerated reading is the capability to read thoroughly but at considerably elevated reading rates. When time is short students need to be able to read thoroughly within the time available. A student needs to be able to engage in accelerated reading by expending more energy and concentration than would be required in usual reading. At these accelerated rates (perhaps 40 percent–50 percent or higher rates) students who are truly fluent in their usual silent reading should be able to maintain their usual 70 percent or higher comprehension levels.

To practice accelerated reading, students could read a conventional reading selection at their independent reading level, while setting a much higher rate of presentation than typically employed during usual guided reading practice. The reading selection might be presented in one of three types of timed displays: a guided, timed left-to-right scanned manner, line-by-line, or full screens. Using the timed left-to-right display mode is the most challenging for there is no opportunity to reread or bypass words as might typically be the case in accelerated reading. In many situations involving accelerated reading, some words will typically be bypassed and a student will use context to maintain good comprehension.

Accelerated reading practice needs to be monitored well. If a student is not truly fluent or efficient (i.e., he or she exhibits comprehension difficulties), accelerated reading practice should be postponed.

CRITICAL/STUDY-TYPE READING

This type of reading is typically the manner of reading in which the student reads subject area material and textbooks very carefully and thoroughly. In this form of reading, the student will typically read portions of the text but at intervals and pause to visualize, analyze, interpret, and appreciate the information being read. In addition, there could be considerable rereading during critical reading to confirm understanding. As a consequence, the overall rate of completion of study-type reading is typically slower than usual reading.

Study-type reading can be accomplished by independent reading of social studies, science, or other subject area selections at a student's independent reading level. Many of these selections will also include illustrations or other graphics to supply additional information beyond what the text can state. Again, the goal of study-type reading is thorough comprehension with as much efficiency as possible.

Study-type reading exercises should start with general goal statements or questions to guide the student with this type of reading practice. These questions may be directed to the assumptions of the author, his or her point of view, the points presented, and the logic of any conclusions.

Study-type reading practice might involve the presentation of full-screen displays with students progressing manually from one frame to the next as they complete their reading of each frame of text. This allows students to study graphics, read all captions, and to reflect on the content of each frame. Thus, there would not typically be any timing in the display of text, but there could be an overall completion time recorded and displayed once the entire selection had been read in order to judge general efficiency and completion rate in relation to usual reading. Timing could be a motivating element as far as the students are concerned as long as they also take note of their comprehension performance. Following this practice reading, there would typically be a certain number of comprehension questions presented relating to the text read and information that could have been derived from any graphics.

SKIMMING

Skimming is an invaluable study skill capability. During skimming much of the text will not be read and many words will be bypassed. This partial reading is required in many study situations where the goal of skimming is to primarily derive the gist of the content, look for specific information, and possibly to make a decision as to whether or not a selection should be read again in a more thorough fashion to fully comprehend all of the information. Skimming, in general, occurs when a student is attempting to move through reading material at overall rates that are 100 percent faster than his or her usual rate of reading. At these elevated rates, it is likely that only portions of the content can be read. Grayum's study (1953) revealed that students involved in skimming typically read sections of content in a usual manner and then skipped portions to move on to new content to be read or skimmed.

Skimming Patterns

In skimming, content read will be dealt with visually in a series of fixations not unlike that of inclusive reading. But at intervals, sections will be skipped, or only portions of sentences will be read. The truly artful skimmer will develop the knack of sensing when he or she has read enough and then quickly move to new content. Therefore, eye-movement recordings of students engaged in skimming typically show patterns of usual reading interrupted by extraordinary eye-movement shifts to new sections of content, partial reading of certain lines, etc.

It is common practice to introduce students to skimming techniques by directing them to try various visual approaches. In fact, students need to learn to depart from an inclusive reading approach and to find new patterns of visual survey that will "work for them" in terms of partial comprehension.

There are two common visual survey approaches that are presented. One is to read the first sentence of each paragraph or the first several sentences, if the content dictates, or up to approximately 50 percent of each paragraph, if the paragraph is long.

Another common practice is to move the eyes along the first line or two of the paragraph and then "float over" the rest of the paragraph, picking up any words, names, dates, or other material of high stimulus value on the way to the start of the next paragraph. During skimming it is critical that the students try to maintain "thread of thought" despite the fact that all of the text will not be read, as depicted in the example that follows.

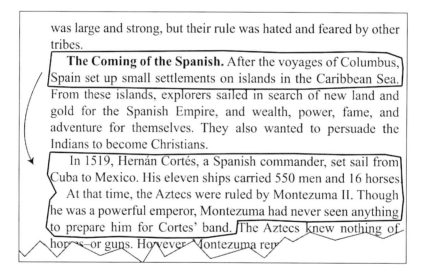

There are two basic forms of skimming practice: overview skimming and preview skimming.

Overview Skimming

To practice skimming, special lessons need to be provided that are at a student's independent reading level. During overview skimming, a selection would be presented in either a timed full-screen display with perhaps a bead of light moving down the page at twice the student's usual rate to establish rate parameters. Following the overview skimming of a selection, a student would be presented with perhaps 15 to 20 statements, and the student would select those statements that were judged to be correct based on the content skimmed.

In overview skimming, the reader intends to derive sufficient information from one high-speed perusal. He or she may not intend to read the article at a later time. As a consequence, in this form of skimming, the reader may read more of the content than in preview skimming, looking for general ideas and organizational features, but also taking note of the more important information and concepts in the content.

The primary difference between preview and overview skimming lies in the intent to read later or not, and in the amount of the article which is read.

Preview Skimming

Preview skimming should be initiated by five or more questions or statements to guide the preview skimming process. The student would fix these questions or statements in his or her mind and then preview skim to find the information as suggested by this preparation. Thus, a student would typically skim through the selection to only locate information related to the questions or statements. Again, a moving bead of light or other timing means could be employed to allow students to know they are maintaining selective reading rates. The same content area reading selections mentioned in study-type reading earlier could be used but with five or so statements or questions presented initially before the student attempts to skim through the selection at 100%+ accelerated rates. The questions or statements would again be presented following the scanning exercise of the entire selection and students would respond to demonstrate acceptable preview comprehension.

Preview skimming is usually undertaken with the awareness that the skimmed content will eventually be read inclusively. In preview skimming, the reader will tend to be particularly attentive to the organization of the content, noting any information or graphics that will help his or her later reading of that content. Preview skimming can provide a good idea of what the author is writing about, what main topics will be covered, the general sequence of major ideas, and the kind of approach used by the author. For example, in preview skimming an article about a scientific topic, the reader can determine answers to questions such as the following:

1. Is the article a very general treatment of the topic or a very detailed discussion?

2. Is the article written in general way, with simple, easy-to-understand language and concepts, or is it more technical, using terms and concepts requiring a great deal of background?
3. Is the article a general discussion of some scientific topic designed to inform the reader, or is the author arguing for a particular point of view or trying to support one particular theory?
4. Does the author seem to be an expert on the topic?
5. How well organized is the author? Does the article follow some obvious plan or structure, or does it ramble all around the topic?
6. How is the article organized and how is the information set forth and arranged?

CONCLUSION

A reading proficiency development program needs to be comprehensive in terms of appraisal, adequate and appropriate content, practice techniques, scaffolding of instruction, and reports of progress to ensure the most individual and effective program for each student. Such a program must not only focus on extended practice as in conventional SSR programs, but also must encompass training techniques that allow students to improve their visual/functional, perceptual, and information processing competence, their vocabulary, and comprehension skill strategies that will eventually qualify them as proficient independent readers. With this competency as a base, students would then need to extend their reading proficiency by reading extensively and learning to apply various reading strategies to become truly effective in the study approaches needed for learning and life.

REFERENCES

Adams, M. J. (1994). Modeling the connections between word recognition and reading. In R. B. Ruddell, M. R. Ruddell, & H. Singer (Eds.), *Theoretical models and processes of reading* (4th ed.), pp. 838–863. Newark, DE: International Reading Association.

Allington, R. L. (2006). Fluency: Still waiting after all these years. In S. J. Samuels & A. E. Farstrup (Eds.), *What research has to say about fluency instruction* (pp. 94–105). Newark, DE: International Reading Association.

Anderson, L. W., & Krathwohl. D. (2001). *A taxonomy for learning, teaching, and assessing: A revision of Bloom's Taxonomy of educational objectives.* New York: Longman.

Betts, E. (1946). *Foundations of reading instruction.* New York: American Book.

Broadbent, D. E. (1975). The magic number seven after 15 years. In A. Kennedy & A. Wilkes (Eds.), *Studies in long-term memory* (pp. 3–18). Oxford, England: Wiley.

Bloom, B., Engelhart, M., Furst, E., Hill, W., & Krathwohl, D. (1956). Taxonomy of educational objectives: The classification of educational goals. *Handbook I: The Cognitive Domain.* New York, Toronto: Longmans, Green.

Carroll, J. B., Davies, P., & Richman, B. (1971). *The American Heritage word frequency book.* Boston: Houghton Mifflin. Dolch Sight Words (n. d.). Retrieved August 7, 2007, from http://www.dolchsightwords.org

Cowan, N. (1993). Activation, attention, and short-term memory. *Memory & Cognition, 21*(2), 162–167.

Cowan, N. (2001). The magical number 4 in short-term memory: A reconsideration of mental storage capacity. *Behav Brain Sci, 24,* 87–185.

Duffy, G., Sherman, G., & Roehler, L. (1977). *How to teach reading systematically.* New York: Harper and Row.

Ehri, L. C. (1995). Phases of development in learning to read words by sight. *Journal of Research in Reading, 18,* 116–125.

Ehri, L. C. (1998). Grapheme-phoneme knowledge is essential for learning to read words in English. In J. L. Metsala & L. C. Ehri (Eds.), *Word recognition in beginning literacy* (pp. 3–40). Mahwah, NJ: Erlbaum.

EyesPlus. http://www.readingplus.com/eyesplus

Grayum, H. S. (1953). An analytic description of skimming: Its purposes and place as an ability in reading. *Studies in Education, Thesis Abstract Series 44.* Bloomington, IN: School of Education, Indiana University.

Hellerstein, L. F., Danner, R., Maples, W., Press, L., & Schneebeck, J. (2001). Optometric guidelines for school consulting. School vision programs–Current updates. *Journal of Optometric Vision Development, 32*(2), 56–75.

Hiebert, E. H. (2006). Becoming fluent: Repeated reading with scaffolded texts. In S. J. Samuels & A. E. Farstrup (Eds.), *What research has to say about fluency instruction* (pp. 204–226). Newark, DE: International Reading Association.

Hill, W. (1963). The influence of set upon ocular-motor and comprehension responses. A paper presented at the Thirteenth Annual Meeting of the National Reading Conference at Loyola University. New Orleans, LA.

Hoover, C. D., & Harris, P. (1997, Winter). The effects of using the ReadFast computer program on eye movement abilities as measured by the OBER2 eye movement device. *Journal of Optometric Vision Development, 28,* 227–234.

LaBerge, D., & Samuels S. J. (1974). Toward a theory of automatic information processing in reading. *Cognitive Psychology 6,* 293–323.

MacNamara, D. S. (2000). *Preliminary analysis of photoreading* (final report). Moffett Field, CA: NASA Ames Research Center.

Maxwell, M. J. (1959). Assessing skimming and scanning improvement. In *The Psychology of Reading Behavior,* 18th Yearbook of The National Reading Conference (pp. 229–233). Milwaukee, WI.

McClusky, H. Y. (1934). An experiment on the influence of preliminary skimming on reading. *Journal of Educational Psychology, 22,* 521–529.

Miller, G. A. (1956). The magic number seven, plus or minus two: Some limits on our capacity for processing information. *Psychological Review, 63,* 81–97.

Mirsky, A. F. (1999). Disorders of attention: A neuropsychological perspective. In G. F. Lyon & N. A. Krasnegor (Eds.), *Attention, memory, and executive function* (2nd printing, pp. 71–96). Baltimore: Paul H. Brookes Publishing Co.

Moore, W. J. (1955). A laboratory study of the relation of selected elements to the skimming process in silent reading. (Unpublished doctoral dissertation). Syracuse, NY.

Morrison, I. E., & Oakes, M. L. (1970). The effect of skimming on reading achievement. Proceedings of the International Reading Association.

Pearson, P. D., & Gallagher, M. C. (1983). The instruction of reading comprehension. *Contemporary Educational Psychology, 8,* 317–344.

Pikulski, J. J. (2006). Fluency: A developmental and language perspective. In S. J. Samuels & A. E. Farstrup (Eds.), *What research has to say about fluency instruction* (pp. 70–93). Newark, DE: International Reading Association.

Pressley, M., Gaskins, I. W., & Fingeret, L. (2006). Instruction and development of reading fluency in struggling readers. In S. J. Samuels & A. E. Farstrup (Eds.), *What research has to say about fluency instruction* (pp. 47–69). Newark, DE: International Reading Association.

Radach, R., Vorstius, C., & Reilly, R. (July 2010). The science of speed reading: Exploring the impact of speed on visuomotor control and comprehension. Paper presented at the annual meeting of the Society for the Scientific Study of Reading, Berlin, Germany.

Rasinski, T. (2006, April). Reading fluency instruction: Moving beyond accuracy, automaticity, and prosody. *The Reading Teacher, 59*(7), 704–706.

Rasinski, T. V., & Lenhart, L. (2007). Explorations of fluent readers. *Reading Today, 25*(3), 18.

Rasinski, T., Samuels, S. J. Hiebert, E., Petscher, Y., & Feller, K. (2011). The effects of silent reading fluency instructional protocol on students' reading comprehension and achievement in an urban school setting. *Reading Psychology.*

Robinson, F. P. (1934). The tachistoscope as a measure of reading perception. *American Journal of Psychology, 46,* 123–135.

Schlange, D. (1999). Evaluation of the Reading Plus 2000 and Visagraph system as a remedial program for academically "at risk" sixth and eighth grade students: A pilot study. Transactions of the Annual Meeting of the American Academy of Optometry, Pediatric Optometry Poster.

Shiffrin, R., Ratcliff, R., Murnane, K., & Nobel, P. (1993). Learning, memory and cognition. *Journal of Experimental Psychology, 19*(6), 1445–1449.

Taylor, E. A. (1957). The scans: Perception, apprehension, and recognition as related to reading and speed-reading. *AM. J. Journal and Ophth. 44,* 501–507.

Taylor, S. E. (1962). An evaluation of 41 trainees who had recently completed the *Reading Dynamics* program. First Annual Yearbook of the North Central Reading Association, 51–72.

Taylor, S. E. (1964). *Listening. What research says to the teacher, 29.* Washington, DC: National Education Association.

Taylor, S. E. (2006). *Fluency in silent reading.* Winooski, VT: Taylor Associates/Communications, Inc.

Tharp, R. G. (1982). The effective instruction of comprehension: Results and descriptions of the Kamehameha Early Education Program. *Reading Research Quarterly, 17*(4), 503–527.

Thorndike, E. L. (1921). *The teacher's word book.* New York: Columbia University Press.

Torgesen, J. K., & Hudson, R. F. (2006). Reading fluency: Critical issues for struggling readers. In S. J. Samuels & A. E. Farstrup (Eds.), *What research has to say about fluency instruction* (pp. 130–158). Newark, DE: International Reading Association.

Torgesen, J. K., Rashotte, C. P. A., & Alexander, A. (2001). Principles of fluency instruction in reading: Relationships with established empirical outcomes. In M. Wolf (Ed.), *Dyslexia, fluency, and the brain* (pp. 333–355). Parkton, MD: York Press.

Wagner, R. K. (1999). From simple structure to complex function: Major trends in the development of theories, models, and measurements of memory. In G. R. Lyon & N. A. Krasnegor (Eds.), *Attention, memory, and executive function* (2nd printing, pp. 139–156). Baltimore: Paul H. Brookes.

Zeno, S., Ivens, S., Millard, R., & Duvvuri, R. (1995). *Educator's word frequency guide.* Brewster, NY: Touchstone Applied Science Associates, Inc.

INDEX

179